ICU
Induced Coma Unconscious
Will You Wake Up?

"I call heaven and earth to record this day against you, that I have set before you life and death, blessing and cursing: therefore choose life, that both thou and thy seed may live"

DEUTERONOMY 30:19 KJV

Lady Mary Hatter

© Copyright 2021, Lady Mary Hatter

All Rights Reserved.

In accordance with the U.S. Copyright Act of 1976, the scanning, uploading, and electronic sharing of any part of this book without the permission of the publisher constitute unlawful privacy and theft of the author's intellectual property. If you would like to use material from the book (other than for preview purposes), prior written permission must be obtained by contacting the publisher at the address below. Thank you for your support of the author's rights.

ISBN: 978-1-60414-531-1

Visit the author's website for more information:

www.MaryHatter.com

Dedication & Acknowledgement

To my husband, Pastor A.D. Hatter, Two children, Tangeneva, and Tristian. My granddaughter, Maranda, my grandson Josiah, both from my daughter Tangeneva. I love you all dearly.

I dedicate this book to all those who are reading and don't understand right now, this book is dedicated to you also. To all who read, I speak blessings to you indeed. My prayer is that you receive. This is my seed. I sow, so you will grow, and go, and that people will know. Continued blessings to the kingdom, and souls being saved. Blessings, blessings, and blessings always!

Table of Contents

Introduction v
The Light in Dark Places 1
Spiritual ATM 3
Listen Up! 4
Live Out the Gospel of Christ 6
The Glory of the Lord is Here 9
Here, the Lost are Found 12
Enter the Prayer Gate 13
God Woke Me Up with These Words: You are My MC 14
A Place We've Never Been Before 18
Receive Your STUFF 21
Activated Promises From God 23
Receive Double 24
Men Walking Around as Trees 28
WOP 30
Praise God 32
The Blood the Body, and the Believer 34
Pay Attention to Details in God's Directions 34
Stay on my POST 36
Leaving the Past Behind 38
God Wants to Heal You Everywhere You Hurt 41
The Spirit of God 43
Praise & Worship 48
Release Mighty Moves 50
God Wants Us to Join Him 51
Today is a Prophetic Day 52

Warning!	54
Your Soul Magnifies God	55
Supernatural Cleansing	57
Grace and Favor Tours	60
Our Enemies are Revealed	64
When God Speaks, Everyone and Every Thing Listens	66
TMI	68
Let Praises Rise	70
Eight Things that Come When You're Obeying the Will of God	72
God's Servant	74
God's Gift of Life	77
You're surrounded by His glory!	79
Pray Without Ceasing	81
Appreciate the Gift	83
Wake Up, Receive Your Stuff	85
Continual Worship!	87
Rest, Jesus, Rest	89
In the Name of Our Savior Jesus Christ	91
Release the Restraints	94
Mighty Victorious Believers' Prayer	96
Conclusion	100
Sneak Peek at *Dreams*	104

Introduction

God is truly amazing! Here we go and grow again! He's blessed us, and we will continue to win! Hallelujah! I'm forever grateful and excited that God keeps blessing me to put His messages out in all forms of communication. In this book you will see how He's blessed me to bless the nation, in this form of communication. In this book *ICU, Induced Coma Unconscious,* I ask these important questions?

1. Do you think it's time to wake up and give your life to God?
2. How will you wake up?

I will share what God has spoken in my times of going into the Courts of Heaven, and how to function properly in the Kingdom of God. When we do this, we receive His insight, His impartation, and His information on how He uses our thoughts, by way of His Holy Spirit, to explain what He wants to do through us, for us, and what He wants to get to us.

In the world when a person is moved to the ICU (Intensive Care Unit) it means their health is at a critical stage. In this particular room, you have to be monitored closely, and things are so serious that some people might not make it out of this room.

Well, in this book we'll discuss the crucial state in the believer's life, where he or she must carry out the mission of Jesus Christ. We must know that it's time to wake up to the things God wants us to see and do and walk in our purpose. Will you make the decision to wake up and obey Him?

Will you put God's teachings into practice by doing the work He's called, commissioned, and commanded you to do?

God spoke the name of this book to me, as He always does before He reveals the contents of my next book to me. I have a daily devotion, where I set aside some time in the early mornings to listen totally to Him. I invite Holy Spirit in daily. In the spirit realm, we have to choose to go in without being distracted. We cannot let demonic forces cause our minds to deviate from our purpose or be disturbed in our devotion. We must set our hearts and minds to fellowship with Him. We must choose to receive from God's Holy Spirit — to be dead to the things of the world, and alive in Christ Jesus.

Even so, consider yourselves to be dead to sin [and your relationship to it broken], but alive to God [in unbroken fellowship with Him] in Christ Jesus.

ROMANS 6:11 AMP

"And you [He made alive when you] were [spiritually] dead and separated from Him because of your transgressions and sins,"

EPHESIANS 2:1 AMP

"And He raised us up together with Him [when we believed], and seated us with Him in the heavenly places, [because we are] in Christ Jesus,"

EPHESIANS 2:6 AMP

The subtitle of this book, Induced Coma Unconscious needs some explanation. Induced means to cause something to come about, like being in a coma, where you are unconscious but not dead. When we allow Holy Spirit to help us we must focus our thoughts on God. We must mediate daily on His word. When we receive the benefits from His wisdom, this shows us how we should live our lives. We should be experiencing and enjoying everything He's already given us by grace though faith.

We don't have to be in bondage or live in brokenness and be broke. God says we make our way prosperous and have good success. We should always choose to make something happen in our lives. We were made to have dominion, be fruitful, multiply, subdue, and replenish. This is our God-given makeup! I've chosen to receive my makeup! Have you?

Women, most of us like to put on makeup and enhance our beauty. Well, I've chosen to use this as an example of what our Father God wants us to do. We must understand and know that we have a choice in the matter. God loves us, so He helps us make that choice. The choices we make aren't just for ourselves, however; they're also for someone else. You want to look good and for others to see you and say how beautiful you look. You don't want to be caught out in public looking a mess. We should be mindful of how we are dressed both in clothing and spirit.

See this scripture:

Do you not know that your body is a temple of the Holy Spirit who is within you, whom you have [received as a gift] from God, and that you are not your own [property]? You were bought with a price [you were actually purchased with the precious blood of Jesus and made His own]. So then, honor and glorify God with your body.

1 CORINTHIANS 6:19-20 AMP

We should want to enhance, increase, and improve in our value, our quality, our desirability, or attractiveness both physically and spiritually. This is our chosen makeup that He's given us. I have chosen to partner with Holy Spirit, obey God, and enter into the Courts of Heaven and see what He's speaking to me by way of His Holy Spirit and then provide that information to you in this book.

The Courts of Heaven and the glory of God is all that He is, all that God has, and all that He's done, and will continue to do. We must know how to enter in, and receive information, and return with instructions. We must rely on what He's imparted in us. This will help us benefit beyond what we see, and what the world sees right now. Stay tuned and let me show you how.

When you enter into the Courts of Heaven, Holy Spirit must always be with you. He must lead and guide you at all times. If you don't allow your mind to think the thoughts that He gives you, this will make your mind not to be in line with Christ Jesus. Let this scripture be your guide:

> "Let this mind be in you, which was also in Christ Jesus:"
>
> PHILIPPIANS 2:5 KJV

Courts of Heaven and the Kingdom of God

First, what do we mean when we say the phrase "Courts of Heaven"? In this case, courts is referring to the court of the Lord, where He is Judge. This is where believers have access, by way of prayer and petition and through intercession by the Holy Spirit who intercedes for the believer, to the Courts of Heaven. Because of the injustices happening in the world, God is releasing new revelation about gaining justice through the Courts of Heaven. The Cross of Christ is our verdict but sometimes we need to enforce this by entering into God's justice system. There are six Courts of Heaven:

1. **The Court of Reconciliation:** [18]*But all these things are from God, who reconciled us to Himself through Christ [making us acceptable to Him] and gave us the ministry of reconciliation [so that by our example we might bring others to Him]* — 2 Corinthians 5:18 AMP

2. **The Court of Petition.** We already operate in the court of petition when we bring our prayers to the Lord: [6]*Do not be anxious or worried about anything, but in everything [every circumstance and situation] by prayer and petition with thanksgiving, continue to make your [specific] requests known to God.* — Philippians 4:6 AMP

3. **The Throne of Grace.** Our interactions with the Lord in the Courts of Heaven should center around prayer and intimacy. We

should approach with grace and mercy toward others: *¹⁶Therefore let us [with privilege] approach the throne of grace [that is, the throne of God's gracious favor] with confidence and without fear, so that we may receive mercy [for our failures] and find [His amazing] grace to help in time of need [an appropriate blessing, coming just at the right moment].* — Hebrews 4:16 AMP

4. **The Court of Mount Zion.** Throughout the Bible, Mount Zion is God's place of justice and judgment. This best describes the Courts of Heaven and how we can approach the Lord: *²²But you have come to Mount Zion and to the city of the living God, the heavenly Jerusalem, and to myriads of angels [in festive gathering], ²³and to the general assembly and assembly of the firstborn who are registered [as citizens] in heaven, and to God, who is Judge of all, and to the spirits of the righteous (the redeemed in heaven) who have been made perfect [bringing them to their final glory], ²⁴and to Jesus, the Mediator of a new covenant [uniting God and man], and to the sprinkled blood, which speaks [of mercy], a better and nobler and more gracious message than the blood of Abel [which cried out for vengeance].* — Hebrews 12:22-24 AMP

5. **The Court of the Accuser.** It is important for us to not operate in the court of the accuser like satan often does in the Bible, but instead come from a spirit of forgiveness and reconciliation: *...For the accuser of our brothers and sisters, who accuses them before our God day and night, has been hurled down.* — Revelation 12:10 AMP

6. **The Court of Ancient Days** (heaven's equivalent of the Supreme Court). This is the highest court and you cannot go in, you must be taken there through visions and dreams. This is not a place to present your case. *⁹"I kept looking until thrones were set up, and the Ancient of Days (God) took His seat; His garment was white as snow and the hair of His head like pure wool. His throne was flames of fire; its wheels were a burning fire.¹⁰A river of fire was flowing and coming out from before Him; a thousand thousands were attending Him, and ten thousand times ten thousand were*

> *standing before Him; the court was seated, and the books were opened* — Daniel 7:9-10 AMP

Remember, you must ask God's permission before operating in the Courts of Heaven.

God governs His court system in Heaven as the sovereign Judge. He hears our circumstances and answers us according to His governmental system. Paul entered the courts of Heaven and charged Timothy before God as judge and the Lord Jesus. Look at this scripture:

> *"I solemnly charge you in the presence of God and of Christ Jesus, who is to judge the living and the dead, and by His appearing and His kingdom: preach the word [as an official messenger]; be ready when the time is right and even when it is not [keep your sense of urgency, whether the opportunity seems favorable or unfavorable, whether convenient or inconvenient, whether welcome or unwelcome]; correct [those who err in doctrine or behavior], warn [those who sin], exhort and encourage [those who are growing toward spiritual maturity], with inexhaustible patience and [faithful] teaching."*
>
> 2 TIMOTHY 4:1-2 AMP

Even through we are suppose to know how to receive from the Courts of Heaven and live according to the Kingdom of God, we understand that some people won't do this because they don't understand or they just don't want to. Will you gain understanding?

1. How will you wake up to the things from God and live the life He's promised you?
2. Will you truly put God first in your life by letting go of what others think of you and giving yourself a voice? Love is putting God first by giving yourself permission to be you.
3. Can you set boundaries and respect yourself? When you deny who you are, it's like saying God made a mistake when He created you.

The Courts of Heaven, according to the scriptures, is where you receive revelations from listening to the voice of God by way of His Holy Spirit. For those of you who want to, by all means keep listening in. In this book, as I'm led by Holy Spirit I will show you how and what to do.

Note: Functioning in the Unshakable Kingdom of God. Look at these four key words that will assist us in operating properly.

Taken from Hebrews 12:25-29 AMP

1. **Speaking:** In verse 25 God is speaking to the believers now. We see an unmovable kingdom. The church should be in this kingdom. If we as believers in our churches don't function properly or outside of the ordinary, we will become just a social gathering. The world should see a difference in us, and want to receive what we have, which is better and extraordinary blessings. We should be asking God to speak to us and give us directions in our lives. The worse thing we can do is copy off someone's paper that was wrong. We shouldn't follow after the worlds example, however follow the word of God.

2. **Shook:** In verse 26 His voice shook the earth. This is our assignment as believers. Notice I keep saying believers? We are called Christians; however, we must believe, have faith, trust, lean, rely on God, without any sense realm evidence that He has allowed it all to come to pass. This is what happens when heaven and earth move together.

3. **Shaken:** Notice verse 27 God is doing a final removal and transformation of all things that was created, and that can be shaken, and He's making them unshakable. Rooted and grounded in Him, and in Christ Jesus.

4. **Serve:** Finally in this 28th verse our seeing, hearing, and understanding, should be with reverence to our almighty God, which causes us as believers to fear Him only. We should possess the mindset that the kingdom must keep moving. As believers we must set our minds on going into the Courts of Heaven to receive

revelations, and keep functioning properly, which is according to the Kingdom of God and His righteousness. In doing so we shall rest, rule, reign, and remain in the all supernatural surplus, and all sufficient things from His Spirit, in heavenly places, released here on earth.

There's a danger in not functioning properly in the Kingdom of God, as mentioned in this scripture:

> *"See to it that you do not refuse [to listen to] Him who is speaking [to you now]. For if those [sons of Israel] did not escape when they refused [to listen to] him who warned them on earth [revealing God's will], how much less will we escape if we turn our backs on Him who warns from heaven? His voice shook the earth [at Mount Sinai] then, but now He has given a promise, saying, "Yet once more I will shake not only the earth, but also the [starry] heaven." Now this [expression], "Yet once more," indicates the removal and final transformation of all those things which can be shaken—that is, of that which has been created—so that those things which cannot be shaken may remain. Therefore, since we receive a kingdom which cannot be shaken, let us show gratitude, and offer to God pleasing service and acceptable worship with reverence and awe; for our God is [indeed] a consuming fire."*
>
> HEBREWS 12:25-29 AMP

When you know who, what, where, and how, you can see what God has for me and for you. Let's enter in, let us show you how to win! Us, meaning Holy Spirit and me. Remember, He's the one to trust! Listen up!

The Light in Dark Places

OCTOPUS

Eight million
New beginning

Like the Octopus, you have eight legs of strength.
Grace
Mercy
Faith
Righteousness
God's heart
Wisdom
Obedience
Prophetic Anointing

You have eight million to start, and many millions that are coming. Know that you have plenty of money. Abundance is never a problem. Remember this, "Anytime you think you can't do something, know that I've already made it happen for you. Never have any doubt that you are out. You are out of lack and limitations, lack and poverty. You have been brought into wealth, and riches now. What you thought you couldn't afford — the house is yours. I've opened the doors. Enter into My gates with thanksgiving, and into My courts with praise. Always be thankful and bless My holy name: the name above every name, the name that never changes.

You have My heart. You've been given a new start. Where you began, isn't where you now stand. Your position has changed. Bless His holy name. Use your eight legs of strength. You've been sent, because I've told you to repent. You obeyed. You will never go astray. Keep going My way. The way has been made even when you couldn't see the way.

Today is always your day. Your blessings are here to stay. The price has been paid. Again, you obeyed. Unlimited books are being sold. People are doing what they were told. Your money they will not withhold.

My Word is spoken through you, they are reading and receiving. You are reaping the harvest I've promised. You know it's not just about money. Souls are coming from the north, south, east, and west. I've chosen the best. People have passed many tests. What you've decreed, you have received, know that it has all come from Me.

When I close my eyes again, after I've been in the Courts of Heaven, I see what looks like a dark door with light all around it. Spirit says to me: "You are the light in dark places. Always let your light shine for all the world to see, they will know this light you have, comes from Me. My glory is revealed."

Spiritual ATM

Will Bearer
Cupbearer
Master Angel
New Home Toll-brothers
ATM Machine
Extra Large Silver Barrel
Glory of the Lord
Women going to their cars parked on busy street like New York

Jesus is the Will in the middle of the Will. You are the bearer, or you possess the Will of God. You follow God with all your heart. Let nothing cause you to depart. You are the Cupbearer, your cup runs over.

The Master Angel has brought you into your New Home. He had to activate the presence of a host of angels for you to receive the unlimited abundance that's coming everywhere you are, and everywhere you go — and you won't have to go far. God has removed the bar.

The Spiritual ATM Machine is in. It's been placed everywhere you go, and everywhere you are. You continue to make withdrawals, and deposits. You continue to withdraw from the seeds you sow. You posses Extra Large Silver Barrel of abundance, because the glory of the Lord has come in.

When His glory comes in, people will begin to move, get busy, getting into their cars, going to their destinations without hesitation. The glory takes you to a large place with lots of traffic — like New York City. When the glory comes in, this is an awesome time and place where everyone wins. No sins.

God's power has been released. His revelations never cease. Move your feet. Praise Him from glory to glory. Tell your story, your testimony. To God be the glory. You go in one way, and come out another way. This way seems right to man, but it's not in God's plans. That's the first way. You come out as pure gold. Blessings, after blessings have unfolded. His glory, behold.

Receive always, and thank Him with praise. Worship God in spirit and in truth. Now you know what to do. The Courts of Heaven are opened for you. Enter in, see what's within. The verdict is in. You win. You never loose, when it's God you choose.

It's your choice to make His Will become your Will. Be still, know that He's God. He has the plans in His hands. Expect and receive the plans He's given to man and woman. It's all good, because you stood.

For I know the plans and thoughts that I have for you,' says the LORD, 'plans for peace and well-being and not for disaster to give you a future and a hope.

JEREMIAH 29:11 AMP

Listen Up!

When you give your life to Christ you can begin to learn how to seek peace and live peacefully. You don't have to be misguided by fake people and false prophets. You will find you can make the best of difficult situations. To give your life to Christ do the following:

1. Trust Jesus Christ.
2. Admit you are a sinner and need God's help: ...*all have sinned and continually fall short of the glory of God* — Romans 3:23)
3. Be willing to change your mind and turn away from sin: "*I tell you, no; but unless you repent [change your old way of thinking, turn from your sinful ways and live changed lives], you will all likewise perish.*" — Luke 13:5 AMP
4. Believe that Jesus died for you, was buried, and then rose from the dead: *But God clearly shows and proves His own love for us, by the*

fact that while we were still sinners, Christ died for us. — Romans 5:8 AMP

5. Invite Jesus into your heart through prayer, and ask Him to become your personal Lord and Savior: *For "whoever calls on the name of the Lord [in prayer] will be saved."* — Romans 10:13

6. Pray the following: Dear God, I am a sinner and need forgiveness. I believe Jesus Christ died for my sins. I am willing to change and turn from my sin, and I invite Jesus Christ to come into my heart and life as my personal Savior.

because if you acknowledge and confess with your mouth that Jesus is Lord [recognizing His power, authority, and majesty as God], and believe in your heart that God raised Him from the dead, you will be saved. 10 For with the heart a person believes [in Christ as Savior] resulting in his justification [that is, being made righteous—being freed of the guilt of sin and made acceptable to God]; and with the mouth he acknowledges and confesses [his faith openly], resulting in and confirming [his] salvation.

ROMANS 10:9-14

Live Out the Gospel of Christ

I saw the judge hit the gavel. I heard "not guilty." I saw the handcuffs and chains removed. I heard, "Go ye therefore." I ran out of the courtroom. I see that people have been released from their sins. The things that held them captive have been removed, never to come back again. They must go and tell the world about what God has done for them.

They have won, because God has sent His son. Go and live out the Gospel of Christ. Spread the report — the good news of the Gospel. The death, burial, and resurrection of Jesus Christ, this is the life. Teach and tell the testimony of how your life changed when you were released from the chains of sin. In Christ Jesus you shall remain.

Reach others by telling your story. To God be the glory! This is your purpose. You must precede, because God has already met your need. You are inspired, continue to acquire, receive your desires. Obey, pray, and stay, because in this place God keeps making away. Never go astray. This is the only way.

Keep running for and with Jesus. You are made in His image. What you see is what He's allowed to come into your imagination. Your dreams have come alive. Always live in Christ Jesus. Your sins were forgiven, for this very reason. Dead to sins, alive in Him. Enjoy life! Always live knowing Christ is alive, living on the inside.

Display Jesus. Let Him show up on the outside — inward worship, with outward praise. Bless His Holy name! Worship God in spirit and in truth. He seeks those to worship Him, and he's chosen you.

God is a Spirit: and they that worship Him must worship Him in spirit and in truth.

JOHN 4:24 KJV

As I go into the courts of Heaven today, this is what God revealed to me, by way of His Holy Spirit. I began to see this one-story house with a long walkway going to it. There was greenery all around the house. The house also had a small body of water on the sides and the back of it. This represents the path leading us through the green pastures and beside the still waters.

He maketh me to lie down in green pastures:
he leadeth me beside the still waters.

PSALMS 23:2 KJV

The next thing I saw was a large body of water with a bridge going across it, with smoke all around the water. Holy Ghost revealed that this is a representation of the supernatural substance from God that shows His glory being revealed. With all this water there was a calmness and peace. The waters didn't have any waves and it wasn't overflowing or flooding the house or moving fast under the bridge.

God says to us: peace, be still. He wants us to wait on Him to reveal what's in store for us is for real. The enemy can't and won't be able to steal. Stay calm in the storm, it won't be long — this storm of not seeing the manifestations yet, this storm of not living in the overflow and outpouring of blessings yet, won't be long. Remember, I've caused the breaking of the nets. Again, it won't be long now, God decrees, if you keep following Me.

If you obey all the decrees and commands I am giving you today,
all will be well with you and your children. I am giving you these
instructions so you will enjoy a long life in the land the Lord your God
is giving you for all time.

DEUTERONOMY 4:40 NLT

The harvest you will soon see, and know it's all from Me. Man couldn't give you what I have revealed. Your blessings have come from the field. The white fields have already been harvested.

Say not ye, There are yet four months, and then cometh harvest? behold, I say unto you, Lift up your eyes, and look on the fields; for they are white already to harvest.

JOHN 4:35 KJV

Plenty, plenty, and plenty of harvest is coming. Because you have waited patiently, again you will soon see. Receive from Me. Never worry about what people see and say, know that I've caused these blessings to come and keep coming your way, and they are here to stay. What man gives, he can take away. No one can undo what I've done.

You have victory and vindication because of My son. Be happy in Christ Jesus. Continue to live in Me. My Holy Spirit shall keep revealing and you will continue to see everything that comes from Me.

Again, receive, receive, and receive, all these enormous blessings from Me: your almighty, all-powerful God of all. Keep obeying Me and you will never fall. Enjoy the ride. I shall always provide.

My spirit is always in, with, and working through you. Remember, as long as you are in Me and I am in you, the devil does only what you let him do. Because you had peace and calmness in the storm, you have come through with all these blessings I've promised you.

The Glory of the Lord is Here

I see clouds all around falling from the sky. Lots of people walking fast towards me. There's a long, narrow, never-ending path with water on both sides. There's a white fireplace, that represents the Holy Ghost fire that's falling when the glory comes. The glory of the Lord is here. He's in this atmosphere.

When God's glory shows up, it's like clouds clearing from the sky. God's people are drawn toward the glory, so they can be in His presence. Quickly and suddenly is how this should be. All things shall come to me if I keep believing, trusting and obeying God. Do this and you will soon see.

Your time has come. Victory has been won. The outpouring and overflowing of God's blessings has begun. You have kept the faith, and everything is moving your way. The building you shall soon be in, know that it's a blessing from within.

Worship God from the inside and receive on the outside. Within is where God resides. On the outside is where you see what He has provided. Keep allowing Him to abide on the inside.

"If you remain in Me and My words remain in you [that is, if we are vitally united and My message lives in your heart], ask whatever you wish and it will be done for you."

John 15:7 AMP

You have favor, take the step in authority and move into your blessed place — the large place that God has promised. The calls have come in, and you win. Now is the time to enter in. The gates are open, and

God has spoken. You have and continued to praise God, even when the people can't see.

Now, enter into His gates with thanksgiving, and into His courts with praise, and continue to bless His Holy name. Your life will never be the same. Don't be afraid to take the step in authority, because God has already made the way. This is the long, narrow, and never-ending path with water on both sides. This is the supernatural supply and surplus that He has promised to His special called-out servants who are willing and obedient.

This is the good of the land, that's in His plans. Plans for you to prosper and have His expected end. Never cease to serve God and His people. Never cease to seek His Kingdom first and His righteousness, and all things shall keep being added to you.

"But first and most importantly seek (aim at, strive after) His kingdom and His righteousness [His way of doing and being right—the attitude and character of God], and all these things will be given to you also."

MATTHEW 6:33 AMP

These are God's promises. Say yes, agree, and all His promises shall be. Now, receive.

"For as many as are the promises of God, in Christ they are [all answered] "Yes." So through Him we say our "Amen" to the glory of God."

2 CORINTHIANS 1:20 AMP

Know this: The light switch has to be turned on in order for the darkness to go away. Light has to shine through darkness to become day. Darkness can't stay when the light is turned on or when light shines through. Light always makes the darkness go away. Whatever your dark situation is, it will soon become day. Joy comes in the morning. Notice it didn't stay night.

For once you were darkness, but now you are light in the Lord; walk as children of Light [live as those who are native-born to the Light]

EPHESIANS 5:8 AMP

How can you find the Glory of the Lord?

1. **Look for the Glory.** If we aren't actively looking for the glory of God, we probably won't see it. Just like anything in God's kingdom, it takes faith to see a manifestation. God's glory is a visible power, and has appeared as a cloud, smoke and fire: *In the sight of the Israelites the appearance of the glory and brilliance of the Lord was like consuming fire on the top of the mountain.* — Exodus 24:17

2. **Pray for the Glory.** How do you do this? First, pray that the glory will be revealed to you and in you. You can see and experience the glory of God, but you must diligently ask and seek it before it will be revealed. Each believer has the ability to manifest God's glory here on earth. When we pray the glory into the earth, miracles and signs will occur in the church and in our lives: *17[I always pray] that the God of our Lord Jesus Christ, the Father of glory, may grant you a spirit of wisdom and of revelation [that gives you a deep and personal and intimate insight] into the true knowledge of Him [for we know the Father through the Son]. 18And [I pray] that the eyes of your heart [the very center and core of your being] may be enlightened [flooded with light by the Holy Spirit], so that you will know and cherish the [a]hope [the divine guarantee, the confident expectation] to which He has called you, the riches of His glorious inheritance in the [b]saints (God's people),* — Ephesians 1:17-18 AMP

3. **Prepare your spirit.** To do this, walk in love and have faith, because faith only works by love. The glory of God will increase in you in direct proportion to how you walk in love: *For [if we are] in Christ Jesus neither circumcision nor uncircumcision means anything, but only faith activated and expressed and working through love.* — Galatians 5:6 AMP

4. **Walk in the Glory.** The glory of God needs a place to dwell. Under the New Covenant, Holy Spirit builds a temple in every believer: *Do you not know and understand that you [the church] are the temple of God, and that the Spirit of God dwells [permanently] — in you [collectively and individually]?* — 1 Corinthians 3:16 AMP

Here, the Lost are Found

I see green trees all around. A bench and a table. It looks like a park, and a large open space. People shall recognize the large place they are in. We are seated at the table where we always win. This is a place of fun, growth, and no worries.

Only God's elect can enter in this place. This place we have never been before. Open place, enclosed. Where it ends isn't where it begins. We can move about freely, with no restrictions. This place is God's great mission. We've been set in this position. At the table of triumph and treasure. Faith without measure.

This place we didn't pay to get in, because the price was already paid for us. This place is for God's Righteous Servants.

We are receiving Supernatural Meals for the homeless and hopeless. Homeless meaning not having a place but wanting to go to a place where there's rest and restoration. Hopeless meaning not having hope but hope being built on nothing less than Jesus Christ and his faithfulness.

> "And in accordance with this will [of God] we [who believe in the message of salvation] have been sanctified [that is, set apart as holy for God and His purposes] through the offering of the body of Jesus Christ (the Messiah, the Anointed) once for all."
>
> HEBREWS 10:10 AMP

We all can enter into this place, as long as we obey the One who made this place, and made it available to us. He is the true and living God. He's never far. He's always around, for the lost to be found. If they want to enter in, sin can't abound. We must help those that want to come in, and show them how to get in, and win. Jesus is the way, truth, and the light. We must love Him with all our might.

"Jesus said to him, "I am the [only] Way [to God] and the [real] Truth and the [real] Life; no one comes to the Father but through Me."
JOHN 14:6 AMP

Enjoy and be exceedingly glad!

Enter the Prayer Gate

1. Entrance Permission...throne of grace...the way into the Kingdom of God

2. Ending Poverty...Tithes and giving...that they want to tap into the Kingdom of God

3. Encouraging People...touch and grab...seize attention to bring them into the Kingdom of God

4. Expecting Prosperity...trusting God, respecting and obeying His instructions, therefore, we all receive what's already been released by Him, and His Kingdom.

God Woke Me Up with These Words: You are My MC (master caller)

God has brought us into a land that flows with milk and honey, and plenty of money. A land of brooks, hills, and fountains. He has removed all mountains. Marinate and mediate on God's Word daily. Respect Him by following His instructions, and expect Him to bring it all to pass.

> *"If the LORD delights in us,
> then He will bring us into this land and give it to us,
> a land which flows with milk and honey."*
>
> NUMBERS 14:8 AMP

"For the LORD your God is bringing you into a good land, a land of brooks of water, of fountains and springs, flowing forth in valleys and hills; a land of wheat and barley, and vines and fig trees and pomegranates, a land of olive oil and honey; a land where you will eat bread without shortage, in which you will lack nothing; a land whose stones are iron, and out of whose hills you can dig copper. When you have eaten and are satisfied, then you shall bless the LORD your God for the good land which He has given you."

DEUTERONOMY 8:7-10 AMP

"But his delight is in the law of the LORD, And on His law [His precepts and teachings] he [habitually] meditates day and night. And he will be like a tree firmly planted [and fed] by streams of water, Which yields its fruit in its season; Its leaf does not wither; And in whatever he does, he prospers [and comes to maturity]."

PSALM 1:2-3 AMP

"Whoever despises the word and counsel [of God] brings destruction upon himself, But he who [reverently] fears and respects the commandment [of God] will be rewarded."

PROVERBS 13:13 AMP

Words from the MC

What I call will come because it's His will that has been done. Everything I call, I must say because I'm a Master Caller, and I have called because it's according to God's will and it's already done.

I believe, I've received, and I thank God for it. In Jesus name, it's done. Angels bring it to me now.

Before I went into the courts of Heaven, I commanded certain things to come, and Holy Spirit instructed me to say what God spoke to me beforehand.

This is what I saw after I entered in: Chains wrapped around people, a chainsaw, and a brick building with large, square, glass windows surrounding it.

We have the tools to remove everything that has held us down. Release yourselves now. The church building is ours now. We didn't have to go far, it was always near. We had to get in a place to hear.

You have heard from Me. Take the step now. Go and tell them: "The Lord sent me here." They will know what to do next. It's already done, because it's My will. KMC has been filled. This is the Word from God.

Next, I called deliverance, and living in health for myself and the people. I called for increase, multiplication, and abundance: because I decreed this before, however I wasn't a Master Caller at that time, and God hadn't revealed to me through Apostle Leroy Thompson that I was a Wealth Caller. I'm to start calling things to come. God also revealed I was to call the angels to bring it all to me, after I call things to come.

These words were spoken to me: Levels, Launch, Love, Live, Life, Super-ceded, Soaked, Supernatural , Superb, Sustained, Substance and Supreme.

I've been promoted to higher levels. Launch out with God's love. I will live life according to what He's promised and positioned me to receive, which is His plan that has been given to prosper me, and I've succeeded. I receive. Thank You, Lord!

I have Super-ceded far above the rest, because He made me — I'm His very best. I'm Soaked in the Supernatural, Superb, Sustained Substance, of the Supreme God of all god's.

I respect and expect Him to always move on my behalf: and for others that I intercede for, on their behalf. I will always obey and do what He says. He has given me, and will continue to give to me, the very things He hears and has heard me say.

Every approval I've been waiting on has been granted. My credit scores have increased to the maximum, because this is what the world system requires. God has showed the world, He's given His people what they desire. Nothing will stop us. God says "go ahead world system, inquire." "Check the report, and see the marvelous thing that He's done."

Victory has been won, because of His son, Christ Jesus. We have received because of this very reason. We have already received, and must continue to receive in every season.

We live in miracles, signs, and wonders. Allow the gifts to flow, even when you don't know. Holy Spirit reveals, as God allows you to be the show. People will see the marvelous things that God has done. He will keep allowing these things to come. He repeated it again in His Word, and we shall continue to repeat and call what He's said. Keep believing, receiving, and thanking God for it all.

> *"When these signs come to you, do for yourself whatever the situation requires, for God is with you."*
>
> 1 SAMUEL 10:7 AMP

> *"These signs will accompany those who have believed in My name they will cast out demons, they will speak in new tongues;"*
>
> MARK 16:17 AMP

"I assure you and most solemnly say to you, this generation [the people living when these signs and events begin] will not pass away until all these things take place."

MATTHEW 24:34 AMP

"I assure you and most solemnly say to you, this generation [the people living when these signs and events begin] will not pass away until all these things take place."

MARK 13:30 AMP

"who came to Jesus at night and said to Him, "Rabbi (Teacher), we know [without any doubt] that You have come from God as a teacher; for no one can do these signs [these wonders, these attesting miracles] that You do unless God is with him.""

JOHN 3:2 AMP

Pray this prayer:

Holy Spirit help me to always keep the Predators and Poisonous, Perverted People out my life. Holy Spirit help me to always receive God's Promises, Provisions, Promotions and Prosperity."
Amen

A Place We've Never Been Before

This is what He revealed today. Thank You, Lord! We're in a place that we've never been before. I see us walking through the open doors. The gates are open and we go in. This is a place where we always win. We have permission now and we enter in.

God's Holy Spirit keeps us hearing from within. This is the place that we always dreamed of. This is the place that's sent from heaven above. I'm in this place because of His love.

This place is where I live. This place is where I always give, in Christ Jesus. I'm glad we met. It's never about what I can get. God is not done with me yet. What He's done, and keeps doing, I will never forget.

I worship God in spirit and in truth. I allow Him to use me the way He wants to. I'm obedient to His Word. I'm hearing things I've never heard.

I love God with all my heart. In this place He's positioned me; I will never depart. In this place He's never far. God will bless you where you are. In this place I've topped the bar.

My blessings are unlimited and will last a lifetime. I'm shining in His divine light. People are seeing what an awesome God I serve — all the glory He deserves! My life He has preserved. I Thank Him for it all!

In this place I can't fall. I stay focused, and in faith. I keep doing things God's way. In this place I'm here to stay. Favor continues to find me every day; therefore, I will never stray.

His instructions I follow. I always have hope for today, and tomorrow. In this place I'm the lender, and not the borrower. In this place I have no sorrow.

At the cross Jesus paid it all. Thank God for the cross experience. In Him I have recompense. I thank You, Lord, for the blood that was shed, and You allowing me to be Spirit led. My hope is in Christ Jesus.

I know I'm in this place for a reason. This is my due season. Seasons come and they go. Everywhere God leads me, I will follow. Seasons are throughout the year. I continue to hear.

I got the power. I keep hearing, hour after hour. Satan can't devour this power. I tread over everything that tries to harm me.

Behold, I give unto you power to tread on serpents and scorpions, and over all the power of the enemy: and nothing shall by any means hurt you.

LUKE 10:19 KJV

I'm not afraid of the devil. With this power, God has me on a higher level. Unlimited resources and revenue have been given to me. I continue to receive revelations; therefore, I will help this generation, and generations to come. God's work never ceases to be done. We have won, because of His Son, our Savior.

Don't stop. Keep seeking the Kingdom of God and His righteousness, and all things are added unto you. This is what I do.

But seek ye first the Kingdom of God, and his righteousness; and all these things shall be added unto you.

MATTHEW 6:33 KJV

You will never have to chase after these things; they will find you. Keep obeying, and following the instructions God keeps giving you. He will always come through. In Him there's no failure.

I have been through the stormy weather. Remember the key words are "have been through." Now I'm writing this to you. Water-breaking Faith. There's more help on the way, every day.

Listen up. See what else Holy Spirit allows me to say, as I rely on Him along the way. I know you will stay tuned in. Again, I love this place I'm in — this place where everyone wins.

How can you be in the winning place?

1. **Desire.** Have the desire to live for Jesus, to be like Him and to hear His voice. Do not settle for what the world offers, because that will not last. We must desire to follow Jesus above all else.

2. **Discipline.** Give up anything that interferes with reaching your goals. This type of self-denial is important to your spiritual life. We need to let go of sins and vices, and must exercise our minds so we think on spiritual things and prepare ourselves to deal with the pressures the sinful world puts upon us every day. We must sit down at the table prepared by the Holy Spirit and fill ourselves with the fruit of the spirit so we can gain spiritual strength.

3. **Commitment.** Focus and commitment both determine whether we view being a Christian as a recreation or a way of life. We cannot give up when things become difficult or when we're asked to do something we don't want to do. We must live totally for Jesus.

4. **Teamwork.** Spiritually, we all need to do our part to help the entire body of the church. We need to be involved in others' lives because none of us are immune to temptation. God knows this and gave us our church family to help us overcome temptations.

5. **Winning.** Because of Jesus, we can't lose. God sent his Son to break the hold of sin on our lies and bring us back into a relationship with Him. Satan may try to bring temptation into our lives, but he won't defeat us. He can't win unless we let him. If we trust in Jesus, we will one day receive the heavenly prize God has set for us.

Receive Your STUFF

Jump through the loop. Leap, and take the victory lap. Launch out into the deep, deeper depths. Watch what I allow you to pull up!

    Receive your STUFF:
    Supernatural
    Transference
    Unlimited
    Fruit and
    Finances

Your life will be good — not by chance, but by change. I've allowed all of this to come to you in Jesus' name. Your life has forever changed. Your family shall receive the same. Because you have experienced this lack, you are an example. I'm using your example so that you and others can see that your life in Christ Jesus is definitely on track.

I've given you the power to get the wealth. This wealth I've given you shall receive, retain, and always remain. I couldn't have allowed the manifestations before this time. Time works at My command.

The people and you shall know I've placed it all in your hands. Continue to stand. It's not about man. I've chosen to use mankind.

This wealth has come through My Divine, now shine. This is the wealth that you couldn't find. Money keeps looking for you. Keep obeying and doing what I say to do. All will see it's from Me.

Again, I'm not a man, and I can't lie. Your fruit and finances shall continue to multiply. Supernatural surplus and supply. You will never just get by. You are the apple of My eye.

This fruit I use as an example of the good fruit, even in the beginning. In this present time and no one can pervert or poison what I've made to be for your good. This is all because in the days of adversity you stood, just like I knew you would. Distractions will come, know that you have already won, again, because of My Son.

Supernatural Avenue — this is a special street, divinely made, especially for you. The gates are opened just for you. Drive in, and walk in. Again, this is the place of promises, promotions, and prosperity. I'm repeating to keep reminding you that you need to keep worshipping and praising Me. I will never forsake or leave you. Keep Me in your heart. I'm never far.

Unlimited blessings have been released. Receive. Know that it's all from Me. I'm pleased to prosper you. Enjoy! Rejoice and be exceedingly glad! I've brought you out of the past and into the present, where I've provided promises and the future finances that shall keep coming. This is the Word from Your Almighty, all-powerful God! Keep believing, obeying, and receiving.

Activated Promises From God

This world will change, but your blessings will always remain, in Jesus name. How you began is not where you stand. Because of your small beginnings, you shall always have great finishes. You finish with plenty. You have become, all because you have begun. Nothing starts until you begin, then I've caused you to win.

You have been given the charge to excel far. Your distance has topped the bar. Unlimited destinations for this generation and generations to come. It's My will being done. Listen, hear, see, understand, and do all that I've preserved, positioned, prepared, placed, and planned for you to succeed, and have the expected end. This is how you will always win.

It is My pleasure to give you all of My promises and prosperity. I've given you dominion, even in the beginning. You are subduing, replenishing, and multiplying. You are living in health, wealth, and riches. It shall all continue in your house.

People will see what I've allowed to be. Great and mighty things I've done, and continue to do. All because of My love for you. Remember to always love Me as I love you. Always love each other, as I've shown you how to love when I gave you My Son, Jesus. You are equipped with the Trinity; therefore, you will always have plenty.

The angels are ready and waiting to bring what you say. Always say what you want them to bring your way. Charge them today. I will do for you the very things I heard and keep hearing you say. This is the word from God! Receive.

Receive Double

You have received double. You will build double, without any trouble. I AM the Lord, your God. I never leave or forsake you. Holy Spirit will always lead and feed you. You have been blessed in the cities and blessed in the fields. The preserved and promised harvest is already prepared for you to see and receive. Thank You, Lord, I receive!

The packages have already been opened. (Apostle Thompson) Receive. You have net breaking abundance manifesting to you now. Know that I brought this abundance about. Abundance is in your house now.

Always command, demand, and decree everything that I've given you to already be. You are rich — very rich. Wealth and riches are in your house now. Never doubt. My prophet has spoken everything out and over you. Do just what you heard him say.

Speak what he said from Me. I will give you just what I heard you say. Receive everything I have allowed to come your way. Abundance is here to stay, today and every day of your life. All because you sacrificed.

Your seeds never will go unnoticed by Me. I AM, that I AM, has spoken, and will continue to speak through you, who will hear, listen, and do. Make sure your seeing, hearing, and understanding is always lined up with Me.

Again, net breaking abundance is here. Boats loads of abundance is here. Remember what I've spoken before. Abundance is in you mouth, and it has to be spoken out. Decree and receive now. I AM the Lord, and I change not.

Just because you didn't know how, doesn't mean that I changed My mind. What I've promised has already come to pass. In the moment, within a twinkling of the eye, that's how fast I've allowed your abundance to multiply. Because you obeyed Me when I said give, this is how I command you to live. Live to give, and give to live.

You are My sower, and you have received and will continue to receive seeds to sow in good soil. Never sow in the wrong soil, because you will receive no harvest. Crops can't come up in bad dirt — dirt without nurturing and watering.

I won't give increase without you listening to Me. You must do things descent and in order. In line all the time with Me. You have your verdict. You win, every time. Again, always remember what I've spoken, and obey Me, even in the not knowing.

The abundance has been released, from all those that have heard from Me. Receive now. Angels are bringing it all in now. Remember, it's not up to you to know how. Just receive now.

People will see these marvelous things that I've done and it's marvelous in their sight. It's for all the world to see. You see, you hear, and you understand. I've placed everything in your hands. You have your expected end, and you will always succeed.

Know that this abundance has come from Me. I've increased, imparted, and inspired you indeed. Yes, abundance inspires and never retires. Yes, abundance motivates, and I never make a mistake. Don't think it's strange, because of who, where, and how this abundance came. Know that it's from Me, in Christ Jesus' name.

Your life will never be the same, because abundance came, and it shall remain. No limits. No lid. I see and remember your seeds always. Keep your seeing, hearing, and understanding, in line with Me all the time, and you will keep shining in My divine.

Again, remember, you win, every time. Remember that what I spoke in the beginning was for you to win. You are here because I spoke light to come from the darkness. I made you and gave you charge and control over everything on this earth.

I never lie. I'm not a man. I don't have a change of plans. My plans stand. I've placed them all in your hands. Decree what I've spoken, and the light of my favor shall shine on you, to make you shine for all the world to see. They will see it's all from Me. This is why this abundance didn't come from who you thought it did.

Keep sowing, sower. You are sowing in the right soil. You shall receive even from the spoil. I'm overflowing the oil. Your cup is running over, and pouring out on all that's under you, and obeying what I say do. Your family, friends, and church. The gates are open. Drive in. Enter into the doors that's yours.

You have dominion. You are increasing, multiplying, replenishing, and subduing. I've done My part, keep doing yours. This is the Word, from the one and only almighty, all-powerful God. You must say and receive, and thank God for it all.

Make Sure Your Seeing Lines Up with Me

Look into where I want you to be. Always expect to see all things through Me. Let this mind be in you, which is also in Christ Jesus. You have never seen the righteous forsaken. I've blessed this generation and shall continue to bless generations to come.

Know that it's My will being done. There's nothing new to Me under the sun or in this earth. This earth that I've made and everything about it is full, and fruitful.

You have dominion, you are subduing, replenishing, and multiplying. You will always have more than enough surplus and supply. What you see is now; don't be weary in well doing. When you see shortages and lack, that's just an indication that the increase has been released and you are on track.

Supernatural is here. Have no fear. Stay in faith. Again, I say, Net breaking, boat loads of abundance has come your way today. Keep believing and receiving. Abundance has been released to you now.

Keep seeing. Your eyes have been enlightened. People see who I've called you to be. Receive what you see. I've changed your current status to overflowing, outpouring, always increasing, never decreasing, never lacking anything. Abundance has been released, and abundance just keeps on coming.

Every day, abundance comes your way. Keep looking and seeing. Expect checks in the mail. Expect abundance you didn't know about to continue to flow. Abundance with a find. Abundance that's always on your mind. Abundance you never have to look for because it knows where you are. That's why it has a find.

People continue to release abundance, even right now. The appeal has been won because you are a part of the law suit. Today is the day of seeing all your abundance that has been released. Quickly, suddenly, right now. You see and receive it all now.

Abundance people tried to hold from you, it's all yours because of My love for you. I've given you just what I heard you say. Continue to obey. Again, abundance keeps coming to you when you do what I say to do.

I am the great I AM. Live in My plans. You are prosperous, and you continue to succeed. This pleases Me. Know that it's all from Me. This is the Word from almighty God! Receive. Rejoice and be exceedingly glad.

Men Walking Around as Trees

When you see me you see money walking. When you see me you see money talking. When you see me you see money flying, soaring like an eagle. I'm not flapping my wings, my wings are out stretched, headed for my nest. The babies are already born. The increase has begun. Money has been preserved, waiting on you to get in position. God has given His permission. Receive His money with a mission. (Apostle Thompson) Money has found you. Now you know what to do. It's all ready happening now. You didn't have to know how. Just thank God for bringing it all about. Shout.

And he looked up and said, "I see people, but [they look] like trees, walking around.

MARK 8:24 AMP

Praise Stops My Pain

1. Praise puts me in Position…verse 18
2. Provides me with my Promises…verse 20
3. Pushes me through my Pain…verse 22

My praise has stopped my pain. I have pushed through the pain with my praise. Pain can't remain. I reign in Jesus' name. As my head was hurting, I began to decree the pain out of me. I called it gone. Then I started praising God, believing, receiving, and thanking Him for removing the pain.

I know that the weapons will be formed, but they shall not prosper. Praise is my weapon against the enemy. Praise God from whom all blessings flow! Praise let's me know this pain must go! Thank You, Lord! I praise You forever more!

Keep allowing the praise to come out. Shout! Know without a doubt God has allowed the healing to come about. Sickness and disease isn't from God. Never accept what the enemy brings. God has already given you everything — even healing. Praise God! Thank God! I receive. I'm pain-free!

> *"Jehoshaphat bowed with his face to the ground, and all Judah and the inhabitants of Jerusalem fell down before the LORD, worshiping Him. The Levites, from the sons of the Kohathites and the sons of the Korahites, stood up to praise the LORD God of Israel, with a very loud voice. So they got up early in the morning and went out into the Wilderness of Tekoa; and as they went out, Jehoshaphat stood and said, "Hear me, O Judah, and you inhabitants of Jerusalem! Believe and trust in the LORD your God and you will be established (secure). Believe and trust in His prophets and succeed." When he had consulted with the people, he appointed those who sang to the LORD and those who praised Him in their holy (priestly) attire, as they went out before the army and said, "Praise and give thanks to the LORD, for His mercy and loving kindness endure forever." When they began singing and praising, the LORD set ambushes against the sons of Ammon, Moab, and Mount Seir, who had come against Judah; so they were struck down [in defeat]."*
>
> 2 CHRONICLES 20:18-22 AMP

WOP

(Wind of Praise)

You can't see the wind but you feel and see the after effects of it. When we praise God, we can't see at first or while we're praising Him what the outcome will be. During and after the praise we see what God's will has done because of our praise. I will praise Him like the wind blows and I will receive the flows. Flows of health and wealth. Fruitful flows. Souls being added to the church that we didn't know. Souls that want to be saved.

"praising God continually, and having favor with all the people. And the Lord kept adding to their number daily those who were being saved."

ACTS 2:47 AMP

My praise has activated all my promises, promotions, and prosperity. Because of my praise I live in peace and God is pleased to prosper me. My praise has caused me to enter into my wealthy place. I'm positioned in praise. I take charge as God has allowed me to go far. Far beyond my reach. My reach wasn't enough to receive what's been preserved and provided for me. In my praise Holy Spirit allows me to hear what God says. What He's said I believe all that I read. His word keeps me daily as I've chosen to get out of the bed. All that God has is not just in my head. What I've imagined from Him I have. I praise and I continue to praise. God has called me by my name. I've accepted the call. My praise has made the walls fall. When I enter into my zone, this place that I own, I receive from all my seeds sown. Yes, sowing is key. I have received the keys to the kingdom that's been given me. Praise is what I always do. When I receive, I show all that will receive too. I love this praise. I will forever bless His name. I kneel down in Jesus name. Because of my praise my life will never be the same. I praise my almighty God! The name above every name! His name will never change. I love this Wind Of Praise! This is the place I choose to stay! I accept and I'm anointed to praise. Will you begin to go into this praise today?

Praise God

1. Praise invokes the presence — Acts 2:47
2. Prayer impacted the people — 1 John 5:14-15
3. Prophetic imparts the promotions — 2 Corinthians 20:20
4. Power induces the prosperity — Joshua 1:8

When we Praise God, He adds those who want to be saved to His church daily. We invoke His presence. Now we sit and saturate in the glory of the Lord, as we soak in the supreme supernatural presence. Through prayer, we are impacted, as the people of God, His body of baptized believers.

The voice of the prophetic imparts the promotions that God has already released by grace through faith. I have power that induces the prosperity. Because I obey and serve Him, I'm spending my days in prosperity and my years in pleasure. This pleases our God.

I continue to be willing and obedient and I keep eating the good of the land. I live in His plans and I succeed in all that I set out to do. I love, and live to give. My heart is connected to God's heart. I never depart, because I've been set apart from the start. He chose me. I bear fruit, it multiplies and remains, in Jesus' name.

I continue in this praise that God called me to do. I worship Him in spirit and in truth. I've been chosen for such a time as this. This is the season of His time, timing, and the times that I'm in. I win, every time. I shine in His divine. I continue to have God on my mind. This is a must. He created me to have dominion, be fruitful, multiply, replenish, and subdue. I walk in everything His spirit tells me to do. I live in the trinity, in the divinity. God the father, God the son, and God the Holy Spirit. The three in one has caused me to live as such.

How you can praise God

1. Through prayer. Simply talk to God and thank Him for all he's given you.
2. Honor God. One of the simplest things you can praise is the fact that God is great and good.
3. Let God know the specific things He's done for you that you're thankful for.
4. Praise God even when things aren't going so well. You can still thank Him for every breath and every day and ask him to help you to look ahead to a brighter time.
5. Finally, ask God to continue to bless your life as He has in the past.

How do you praise God even when you don't feel like it?

- When you don't feel like praising God, look up and see the glory God has set in the heavens.
- When you can't find words, look to *the* Word — scripture is filled with worship, especially the Psalms.
- Remember the benefits of praise — it helps you withstand your enemies.
- Praise strengthens us against satan's attacks. We're especially vulnerable when we're discouraged. Praising God builds up our faith.
- Praise silences the enemy. When we're discouraged the devil likes to whisper bad things in our ears. Praising God silences those whispers.

The Blood the Body, and the Believer

Because of the blood of Jesus, I can live free of sin in this body. I am a believer in Jesus Christ, the one who laid down His life as a living sacrifice for me. Thank God I'm free!

I purpose to love Him as He first loved me. I purpose to love others and help them be free. I live in God's will and continue to give. This is how I choose to live.

I'm made in His image. He gave His one and only son. I give my one and only life. Lord I thank You for the sacrifice! I love You, Lord, with my life! I live this life according to Your will. I continue to allow Your will to be done, because of Your son, I've won.

Pay Attention to Details in God's Directions

God has set you in the right direction. You won't receive what you desire and what God has already done for you if you deviate from the direction of your appointed destination. You must purpose in your heart, from the start, that you will follow God's instructions properly, as you go the distance.

The devil will always try to distract, deter, and destroy you. He brings discourse and discord. The path that God has set you on is true; if you obey Him you won't be rerouted.

Don't allow anyone to bring conflict and confusion to get you off track. You are in this race for the long haul. You will pass people that have made pitstops when they should have obeyed and kept going anyway.

You must pay attention to details and don't allow satan to make you stray. It's the quick reactions and not the thought-out responses that cause you to make stops that were not on the map. This map was prepared before time existed, and you shouldn't resist it.

Make sure you are consistent without contradictions. This could cause you to lose your confidence, courage, and compassion for this Great Commission. Go ye therefore and bring into the Kingdom of God more and more — more souls.

Blessings unfold as we do what we are told. Obedience is the way. There is another way that we think we should go; however, God has given us His succession plans. If we were going to follow our instructions, we shouldn't have accepted His directions. In others words, we should've never started the journey.

Choose to continue in God's path as He allows His Holy Spirit to lead and guide you in every way, and everyday. You will not go astray. You will never get turned around, or be lost. Jesus has paid the cost, on the cross. He got up from the grave so we can be saved. Never forget the cross experience.

Your destiny has already been set. Pay attention to details in God's directions and you will make it to your divine destination of destiny. Receive and enjoy!

Stay on my POST

Position
Obedience
Speaking
Trusting

I've been placed in this Position of Obedience and my speaking is in line with what God's will is for my life. I'm trusting Him with my life continually. I decree everything He wants and wills for me to be. God has given me this POST and I keep receiving the most.

Holy Spirit continues to assist me in all that God has planned for me to be. I'm set, secure, and stationed here without any fear. This is my large place of promotions and prosperity. All because it's His pleasure to prosper me. Everything He has belongs to me. Everything that I am is what He made and wants me to be. I receive now this prosperity. No one can take it from me. I'm forever grateful for this Position that God has me in.

My Obedience is key to my hearing, seeing, and understanding. My eyes are enlightened to the things of God. This is why I excel far. My Speaking is decreeing at all times what I want and not what I don't want. I decree God's will for me. I decree and I purpose in my heart to do everything according to His will. I'm holy, which means I've been set apart. I keep trusting Him. My praise and worship have set me on this POST. When I praise Him, it's my outward invitation for the worship that's on the inside of me to release what He wants to come from me to Him. I worship Him in spirit and in truth. I'm free to do what He wants me to do. I love this place that I'm in. The verdict is in, and I win. Every time. This is my shine.

Now I shall continue to walk in God's Divine. His Trinity. God the father, God the son, and God the Holy Spirit. I decree, the host of angels are employed to work for me. I decree now, that they are encamped all around and about me. I decree, angels go now and bring everything that's in God's will for me, to me now. I decree I'm right where He wants me to be. On my POST. I'm doing and receiving the most. In Christ Jesus I boast, I believe, and I receive God's blessings that's been given me. Thank God for His grace and mercy. My light continues to shine for all the world to see. I continue in Kingdom building, and my heart and mind is always willing.

My love for God causes me to love people, and to discern who they are. I will never to tricked from my POST. I walk in His wisdom, His ways, His word, and His will for my life. I thank Him for giving His son as a living sacrifice. He was made flesh to live among flesh. He was crucified, he died, and he lives again, for the remission of my sins. Now, I choose to continue to always win. I decree that my love keeps coming from within. I love this place God has set me in. I stay in place, and on my POST. I'm in this Position of Obedience, Speaking God will, and Trusting Him to bring it to pass.

Leaving the Past Behind

I start this message out with a question: Do you want to stay in your past or do you want to move on to your victory at last? Never be defeated because you were cheated. Don't say, "What the heck? I won't ever make it out of this wreck."

You must choose who and what you will loose. I say, "loose those people and things that weren't important or instrumental in your life." You must know that they were meant to be temporary. Some people are forever, and some go through the stormy weather; know that with Jesus Christ they gotta get better.

The past few years have been challenging, and the new year will have some challenges too. You must know that you are equipped for the challenge and changes ahead. You must keep moving forward.

Because of Christ, the cross, and his resurrection, you can never lose. You've been made to win and forgiven for your sins. You can go beyond breakthrough because of who you choose. Choose Christ he's our living sacrifice. He gave up His life, paid the price, for us to live right. Live and obey, because He chose to get up out of the grave.

Each day and every moment is a choice, choose now to rejoice! Be happy and exceedingly glad. This new year will be the best year you ever had! Every year afterwards, you will continue to receive. Living life in the spirit will help you receive the supernatural. Please, by all means, receive everything, in this year.

You will keep increasing in your going out and your coming in. Angels will assist you when you take them off unemployment. Employ them to go and bring everything in this new year. I am speaking only what God has spoken, and will keep speaking it — it is a must.

In Christ Jesus we have to trust, and never be left in the dust. Dust is dirty, it's made and formed: never get stuck in the norm. You will never be normal again. You will always win. Over and over again, see what this year brings.

You have come out on top and you don't have to wrestle or fight for your rights. When you live according to God's will, you will forgive, because He forgave.

He brought you out of the mess you made. No more living in darkness. You are the shining bright light that's been charged, commissioned, and commanded to live right. Walk in the plans, and purpose for your life: the Great Commission, that's right.

Choose to keep bringing people to Jesus Christ. I know you can only bring those who want to be brought, and taught. Introduce people to Jesus, and watch him introduce you to them. You have favor with all mankind. God have put you on people minds. Because of you, Christ Jesus they will find. Don't stop your praise. So many souls will be saved because of the choice you made. Never put Jesus back in the grave. You do this when you act as through you not saved. Watch what you say, continue to obey, and see the blessings of the Lord keep coming your way. Everyday is payday. Power and peace is payday. Promotions and promises are your payday. God pays you for working in His Kingdom, bringing in the lost souls that has chosen to be found. People won't look for what they don't care about losing. You will fix only what you want to be repaired. It's your choice. All that being said; if you have not been introduced to Jesus, allow me to introduce him to you. Will you accept him? If you answered yes, say this with me. I thank God in advance for you! Hallelujah!

PRAYER TO BE SAVED

Dear God thank You for your word. I know without Jesus I am lost. I believe your word and if I ask you to save me and come into my heart you will. Jesus, I give you the throne of my life, I turn my back on my old way of living and from this day forward I choose to please you with my life. I confess with thy mouth the Lord Jesus, and I believe in my heart that God hath raised him from the dead; Now fill me with your spirit and power so

I can live a life pleasing in your sight. In Jesus name thank You, father, for saving me.

That if thou shalt confess with thy mouth the Lord Jesus, and shalt believe in thine heart that God hath raised him from the dead, thou shalt be saved. For with the heart man believeth unto righteousness; and with the mouth confession is made unto salvation.

"For whosoever shall call upon the name of the Lord shall be saved."

ROMANS 10:9-10, 13 KJV

Prayer to Be Filled with Holy Spirit

My heavenly Father, I am a believer. I am your child and you are my Father. Jesus is my Lord. I believe with all my heart that your Word is true. Your Word says that, if I will ask, I will receive Holy Spirit, so in the name of Jesus Christ, my Lord, I am asking you to fill me to overflowing with your precious Holy Spirit. Baptize me in Your Holy Spirit. Because of your Word, I believe that I now receive Holy Spirit and I thank You for Him. I believe that Holy Spirit is within me and, by faith, I accept him. Now, Holy Spirit, rise up within me as I praise my God. I fully expect to speak with other tongues, as you give me the utterance.

Meditate These Scriptures On Holy Spirit....JN 14:10,12,16-17; ACTS 1:8, 2:4, 32-33, 39, **8:12-17, 10:44-46, 19:2, 5-6; 1 COR 14:2-15, 18, 27; EPH 6:18; JUDE 20**

God was preparing us and showing us how we were to leave out of the year 2018.

God Wants to Heal You Everywhere You Hurt

Follow Me, and I will show you just where I want you to be. Trust Me and obey. Hear, listen, and do what I say. Watch Me make away out of no way. I'm here to make it happen for you. I've caused you to have dominion, replenish, to multiply and to subdue. Stand, and be bold, watch things unfold. Jesus loves you, this, you should know. In Christ Jesus you are saved.

Fearfully, wonderfully, this is how you were made. Jump start this year, have no fear. Hit the pavement running. Run away from the things that try and stop you in your tracks. I've caused you to keep your mind in tack. There's no turning back. The past isn't an option. Keep pressing toward the mark of the prize of the higher calling that's in Christ Jesus. Forward movement is My charge, if you want to soar far.

Take a lesson from the eagle. He soars, without discord. He has no doubt about where he's headed. His focused is protecting his nest. His wings are out stretched, there's no letting them down in the soar. He only lets them down when he reaches his destination. He stands strong with power, watching over his nest. Just like the eagle you can soar, and not trust the decoy. You are strong in the Lord, and in the power of His might. Live right. Any other way isn't an option.

Stand in My strength. For you, My grace is sufficient. You have more than enough, even if the road seems rough. You are built to last. Don't wonder if it's gone happen. I've shown you how to make it happen. Never get weary in well-doing. You shall reap without fainting, because the harvest has come. All because you allowed My will to be done. You've won.

I've given you My precious son. Healing, it's done. Your mind, body, and soul, will do what they're told. Keep speaking what's already been promised. You will live where and how you desire to live. In health and wealth. This is what I've promised.

Live in the land of fatness and fruitfulness. Your fruit shall always remain, when you keep doing it all in Jesus name. The name above all names, the name that never change. The name in which you came. Love is how you live. From the heart is how you give. Partner with My Holy Spirit and this is how you will keep living. In GROWTH:

> **G**iving
> **R**eleases
> **O**verflow
> **W**ealth
> **T**rust
> **H**im

When you focus on what brings Me joy, I release what gives you joy. Never except the decoy. The Great Commission is My mission. I've place you in this position. When you work your position, I shall continue to add to you everything you desire.

> *But first and most importantly seek (aim at, strive after) His kingdom and His righteousness [His way of doing and being right—the attitude and character of God], and all these things will be given to you also.*
>
> MATTHEW 6:33 AMP

The Spirit of God

Your sons and daughters shall prophesy...

'And it shall be in the last days,' says God, 'That I will pour out My Spirit upon all mankind; And your sons and your daughters shall prophesy, And your young men shall see [divinely prompted] visions, And your old men shall dream [divinely prompted] dreams;

ACTS 2:17 AMP

To one is given through the [Holy] Spirit [the power to speak] the message of wisdom, and to another [the power to express] the word of knowledge and understanding according to the same Spirit; to another [wonder-working] faith [is given] by the same [Holy] Spirit, and to another the [extraordinary] gifts of healings by the one Spirit; and to another the working of miracles, and to another prophecy [foretelling the future, speaking a new message from God to the people], and to another discernment of spirits [the ability to distinguish sound, godly doctrine from the deceptive doctrine of man-made religions and cults], to another various kinds of [unknown] tongues, and to another interpretation of tongues. All these things [the gifts, the achievements, the abilities, the empowering] are brought about by one and the same [Holy] Spirit, distributing to each one individually just as He chooses."

1 CORINTHIANS 12:8-11 AMP

You will bless your home, KMC, and the Kingdom of God. From around the world and afar. You have topped the bar. People on the radio stations, television stations, social media, and in every way your voice will be heard.

You have more than enough, overflowing, and outpouring. Keep straight. Don't deviate. I can't make a mistake. What I said and promised has come to pass! Victory at last!

You recognized it was time. You are in line. Shine, in My Divine Light. Again, receive this miracle. I've made you a sign and a wonder. People will see these marvelous miracles I've done. They will see and say it's marvelous in their sight. Continue to live right. This is a command. Keep following My plans.

Every commandment that I am commanding you today you shall be careful to do, so that you may live and multiply, and go in and possess the land which the LORD swore [to give] to your fathers.

DEUTERONOMY 8:1 AMP

All these blessings will come upon you and overtake you if you pay attention to the voice of the LORD your God.

DEUTERONOMY 28:2 AMP

It's all in your hands. In the storm, you need to stand. I've blessed man and woman. You have come from the back to the front. No one can stop what I've started. No one can push back what I've allowed to be pressed forward. You've been pressed and made straight for My sake. In Christ Jesus you are strong in the Lord!

Again, I've spoke this before. Walk through the doors. This is a command. Stand, never stumble, keep walking in My command. Again, I'm not a man. I can't lie. I've caused things in your life to multiply. Now, prophesy. Again, this is a command. I've placed it all in your hands. Come forth now. I've heard everything you said. I've given you everything I've heard you say. Keep doing things My way. Obey. As your Apostle spoke, your hearing, seeing, and understanding is in line with Me. Keep receiving the assistance of Holy Spirit and commanding the angels to work for you.

Bless the LORD, you His angels, You mighty ones who do His commandments, Obeying the voice of His word!

PSALM 103:20 AMP

Unlimited angels are on assignment for you. Tell them what to do.

The angel of the LORD encamps around those who fear Him [with awe-inspired reverence and worship Him with obedience], And He rescues [each of] them.

PSALM 34:7 AMP

I've given the people for you to train. Dance in Jesus' name. Dance with the prophesying angels.

"Then I saw another angel flying in midheaven, with an eternal gospel to preach to the inhabitants of the earth, to every nation and tribe and language and people;"

REVELATION 14:6 AMP

Find them and train and trust your new team. The spirit of the Lord is upon you. Again, this is a command. Not from man, but to mankind. I shall continue to command things in your life. Hear wisdom when wisdom speaks, because it's from Me. Keep allowing Holy Spirit to speak through you. Command the angels to go and bring everything to you, because much has been given to you. Now much is required of you. You have what you desired. More will keep coming.

People far and near, will hear, your voice, by way of Holy Spirit, from Me. Rest, rule, and receive in My power. I've revived, and restored in My power that I've given you. I am, that I am has spoken. Believe and receive. Again, this is a command. It's in your hands. Follow My plans.

Teamwork for God

Genesis teaches about God's creation of teamwork. One of his first teams was Adam and Eve. After God created Adam, He saw that Adam needed a teammate to help him through life. Genesis 2:18: "Then the Lord God said, "It is not good for the man to be alone; I will make him a helper suitable for him." King Solomon also recognized the need for teamwork, "Two are better than one; because they have a good reward for their work. For if they fall, the one will lift up his fellow: but woe to him that is alone when he falls; for he doesn't have anyone to help him up." (Eccl 4:9-10). So, there is a need for us to create teams to help us spread the word of the Lord.

Few relationships are as important in God's cause as teamwork. The one desire of Christians should be the salvation of souls. Working toward this goal as a team will allow all members to rise to their full strength as they present God's Word. Are you called to work on God's team?

Here are some tips to build your own team for God:

1. Name a captain. This is someone who will take the responsibility for guiding the group and giving orders, while still being a member of the team. The captain must be willing to take the counsel and suggestions of his team. This is what builds team spirit.

2. Find team members. The best teams do not have people with similar skills — they combine the talents and backgrounds from a pool of diverse individuals and appreciate the gifts that each one brings to contribute. Great teams have people that know their role and appreciate others as well. These people can fill various roles on the team, including: speaker (for events, etc.), writer (for newspaper articles/social media), motivator (revivals, and encouragement for others in the group and outside it), organizer (to plan events and keep the group on track), singers, and even someone who has the gift of sincere, earnest prayer.

3. A common goal. All members of the team must be in agreement as to the goal of the team, and then should work tirelessly toward that goal.

4. Team members should support each other. Paul said, "Let each esteem other better than themselves." As members of God's team, we should also pray for each other, and ask God to keep us happy and confident as we work toward the team's goal.

5. Your team's work should be the visible manifestation of compassion and shared vision as you work to gather souls for God.

The spirit of your team is more important than its size, and every person on your team is important. Each member should not only work to find new souls for God, but also strive to kindle the love of God in each of his or her fellow team members' hearts.

[24]and let us consider [thoughtfully] how we may encourage one another to love and to do good deeds, [25]not forsaking our meeting together [as believers for worship and instruction], as is the habit of some, but encouraging one another; and all the more [faithfully] as you see the day [of Christ's return] approaching.

HEBREWS 10:24-25

Praise & Worship

Invite
Invoke
Inspiration
Impartation
Increase

Praise and worship invite and invoke the presence of God. We bow down to God, inviting Him in and invoking His presence. From Him, we receive inspiration and impartation (the ability to give unto others that which God has given to us) in our praise and worship. We are inspired as we acquire and receive increase in Him. We receive in His presence form His wisdom and His word, so that we can live according to His will.

We say to God, "We love You so, and we give up our ways for Your ways."

All things are revealed when we hear what He's saying. Awesome things are received. What an awesome, powerful time it is in His presence.

We can't hear or receive anything from the enemy when we're in God's presence, as we praise and worship. We block out everything other than what Holy Spirit is bringing. We are receiving in the spirit everything to bring in the natural, to help us live a more excellent life in Jesus Christ.

This is a place we want to stay in for a while. This place of praise and worship with God, and I pour out my heart to Him. He hears and answers me. The angels are encamped around and about me. They are listening and bring in everything I'm speaking. I've prayed and invited Holy Spirit and the angels into this place with me.

This is like fire in my bones. I'm shouting, shaking, and moving my body with anticipation of something great happening immediately. The heavens are open. God is reigning down on me like never before. I make a joyful noise unto Him. I praise Him with a loud shout. All these blessings have already come about. My praise has brought them out. By grace and through faith, it's done.

There are rivers of blessings flowing and flooding in our lives now! Because of our praise and worship, our faith, favor, and abundance has increased. We are excited to obey and do what God says. We are ready, restored, revived, redeemed, and released into God's rest and righteousness.

Praise and worship stop the hands of the enemy and destroys them. I say them because they come as many (Legion). Once the enemy has been stopped, we can live in the increase of prosperity from God. We can have peace, knowing that nothing can stop or separate us from the love of God.

Praise and worship is what I do, and it's what I'll continue to give to You! Thank You, awesome and powerful God!

Here are some tips to help you direct your praise and worship:

1. Ask God what He wants to say during worship.
2. Ask God to remove anything that is keeping you from authentically worshiping Him.
3. Ask God to bring you clarity.
4. Surrender and truly let go of what is limiting you.
5. Just be. God doesn't need you to put on a show for Him, he just desires your needy heart to come to Him.
6. Sometimes you don't have to say a thing. Just let God know you know He is everything.

Release Mighty Moves

Right Mannerism and Motives
Release Mighty Moves
Receive Many Manifestations

When you have the Right Mannerism and Motivations, you Release Mighty Moves in the spirit that causes you to Receive Many Manifestations. Loving God and His People is a must, to receive your STUFF:

    Supernatural
    Transference
    Undeniable
    Faith
    Finances

Our righteous stance will be enhanced because we dance as we are worshipping and praising God. Doing this has gotten us where we are. We never have to look far. God is always near, in this atmosphere. This is where we live. We give and we forgive.

Faith in God, and in His presence we continue to be. Our love is for real. This position didn't come from making a deal. Being God's servant isn't a game. We do all things in Jesus' name. It's never about how we feel, however it is about knowing that we've been filled with His spirit. When we pray in the spirit, we speak revelations that we receive because of our obedience in Christ Jesus.

We trust, lean, and rely on God to always bring His blessings to pass. We have come from the past, as we keep pressing toward the mark for the prize of the higher calling in Christ Jesus. Never look back.

If we never allow things to cause us to get off track, we will never be in lack. We continue to give with purpose from the heart. We worship and praise Him like never before, because He's the one that keeps opening doors.

God Wants Us to Join Him

Join Me
Joy in Me
Just in Me
Justified in Me
Justice in Me
Judge in Me
Job in Me

God wants us to join Him every day, and hear what He has to say. We will continue to see things work for and through us. We must have Joy in Him, and be Just in Him. Seek after no one else.

We are to be Justified in Him. Live according to His will for our lives, and not our own will. You have received Justice in Him. He pays back for the evil that has been done against you. He's the Judge, and it's not your Job to repay.

The battle is His and He has already allowed you to win. The enemy has been destroyed because of your praise. Keep listening, hearing, and doing what He says.

Continue to stand strong against satan. Don't be afraid of what the enemy tries to do. In Christ Jesus he's afraid of you. Stay focused and in faith, watch God, keep making a way. Don't go astray.

"I have loved you just as the Father has loved Me; remain in My love [and do not doubt My love for you]. If you keep My commandments and obey My teaching, you will remain in My love, just as I have kept My Father's commandments and remain in His love.
I have told you these things so that My joy and delight may be in you, and that your joy may be made full and complete and overflowing."

JOHN 15:9-11 AMP

Today is a Prophetic Day

IHOP
Impartation
Instructions
Information which brings
Inspiration

Hear and see what has come your way, today. Receive what He's said, all because you got out of bed. The blessings are no longer in your head.

Dreams you've been dreaming are no longer dreams; they have come on the scene. What do I mean? Because you've done what's important to God, He's released what's important to you.

Abundance comes to you through God's plans.

Sickness and disease have been removed from you. You have been made whole because you've done what you were told.

The lies that have been spoken about you are gone and the truth has come out. Shout!

Today you will sow your biggest seed. The Kingdom of God is blessed indeed, because of your biggest seed.

Know that's it's not about abundance leaving your hands, but it's about abundance coming into your hands.

Have no fear, God is here, in this atmosphere. Believe His prophets, and so shall you prosper.

He's done it before and He's doing it again. He's released the extra large seed for you to sow. You must obey, to allow these blessings to come to you today. When you obey, the blessings will have a place to stay.

You've been praying for something new, and when you release the seed it will be yours. The harvest won't come until the seed is sown. Don't back down because of who's around. You've heard the sound. This is the sound of a rain of abundance.

The rain had to come so the crops could come up. The nurturing was all because you got up. Because of the planting and the watering, you've received the increase.

This isn't an ordinary blessings — it's extraordinary. Receive, and rejoice!

How can you get what you need from God?

1. **Getting versus receiving.** Getting things means you've struggled and put in effort to have them. Getting puts the burden on us to figure out how to make things work out the way we want. Receiving means we're receiving things from God through faith, not works.

2. **God is not for sale.** We cannot buy, earn or deserve Him. His gifts of forgiveness, mercy, grace, favor, and salvation are free. We could never do enough to earn or deserve them, so Jesus paid the price we could never pay and got these gifts for us. We simply have to believe to receive them!

3. **Good works do not earn you God's goodness.** Believing that what you do earns you God's favor is actually keeping you from receiving His blessings.

4. **Get your heart right.** You cannot judge and be critical of others and expect God to look on you favorably. Your motives for doing good cannot be selfish, and you cannot want God to bless you with his gifts if you keep trying to earn them or feel you deserve them.

5. **Ask for forgiveness.** Ask God for His love, forgiveness, mercy, grace and all the other gifts He wants to give to you. Say, "God, bless me. I receive your blessings in my life because You are good."

Warning!

Don't bring the same way of living into a new day or year, because you will receive the same old thing. If people you are in relationships with don't choose to change, don't allow them to make you revert to who you were. Keep obeying, hearing, and listening to Holy Spirit's voice.

You do have a choice. Choose life and not death. Choose the blessings and not the curse. Curse, cancel, and call gone, everything you don't want to own — sickness, disease, brokenness, lack, and wrong mindset. All these are not where God wants you to be. He's made you to be His very best.

Be warned before there's destruction. These warnings come with instructions. God wants you to receive. He's given me His word for us to believe. You've made the choice, so live by His voice. Rejoice!

The enemy wants to keep you down, even though you have risen up from the wrong stuff of your past. I know sometimes the going gets rough, however you are tough. You are a diamond that's all shined up. Keep being as you were made to be.

Your light shines for all the world to see. You will never go alone, when you keep God on His throne. Keep Him over you, by obeying what He says do. Receive all that God brings to you.

Your Soul Magnifies God

>Amazing
>Awesome
>Anchored
>Always
>Attracted
>Allow
>Attached
>Anointed
>Acquire
>Accepted

We all need to say the following: Thank You, God, for being my Amazing God. You are an Awesome God. I'm Anchored in You Always. I'm Attracted to what You Allow me to be Attached to. I'm Anointed to Acquire all Your promises that have been released to me. Thank You. God. I've Accepted Your call, command, and charge, in this Great Commission.

I say use me, God, to get all things through me, that will continue to build up Your Kingdom. I'm willing and obedient and I've purposed in my heart, to do Your good work, that You've ordained and set me apart to do. I magnify You, God, with all my heart and soul.

I bless Your name at all times. You are always on my mind. I serve You all the time, as I continue to walk in Your divine light and shine.

I thank You for Your Trinity, (Father, Son, Holy Spirit) that's been with me from the beginning. I thank You that I'm Your beloved one.

Lord, I thank You for making me victorious, and for all the victories I've won. I'm never a victim, and satan can't poison me with his deadly venom. I have power over scorpions and serpents, and nothing by any means can hurt me. I know the weapons will be formed, but they shall not prosper.

Thank You, God, for I have Your plans of prosperity, and I'm succeeding in all that I do. I'm always open for You to get things through me. Thank You for filling me with Your precious gift of Holy Spirit. I always invite Him to show me everything, and how to serve You every day.

I'm blessed going out and coming in! In Christ Jesus, I always win. Because of Him I'm forgiven for my sins. I'm forever grateful for all the things You continue to do through me. I love You, God, with all my heart. I will never depart. Thank You for setting me apart, and having me on Your mind from the start. Amen.

Supernatural Cleansing

I have received a Supernatural Cleansing. I dance in the spirit and bring things into the natural. I bring my healing, my health, and plenty of wealth. The heavens are open. The rivers are flowing — these are particular rivers that God has allowed everything to flow from. They were flowing when we had none. This is where all our help comes from. Help in the spirit that was here in the beginning, before the earth was formed. Trust God, you can read it in Genesis chapter one.

> *"In the beginning God (Elohim) created [by forming from nothing] the heavens and the earth. The earth was formless and void or a waste and emptiness, and darkness was upon the face of the deep [primeval ocean that covered the unformed earth]. The Spirit of God was moving (hovering, brooding) over the face of the waters."*
>
> GENESIS 1:1-2 AMP

Now that I'm cleansed, I can dance properly in the spirit. I will teach all who want to do the same in Jesus' name. You must hear, listen, and obey. Do what you hear God say. Move in a special way. Your movements are key, if you want to follow me.

I've purposed in my heart to follow Him. Dancing until He comes again. We shall always win. I mediate on God's word day and night; always living right, loving Him with all my might and never losing sight.

Know that we've won all faith fights. I'm the example of the tree strongly planted and fed by the rivers of waters that are flowing. I receive fruit right now in my season. My leaf never dies, and everything I set my mind to prospers and succeeds.

But his delight is in the law of the LORD, And on His law [His precepts and teachings] he [habitually] meditates day and night. And he will be like a tree firmly planted [and fed] by streams of water, Which yields its fruit in its season; Its leaf does not wither; And in whatever he does, he prospers [and comes to maturity].

PSALM 1:2-3 AMP

It's all about Him. The one and only true and living God. He keeps allowing us to excel. Holy Spirit will show us every move. Get in the grove. This is the rhythm of receiving. Reaching, grabbing, and having everything it takes to make what the Maker made.

What was made is about Jesus when He got up out the grave. He made death get out of the way. So is Jesus, so are you. You are made in His image, too.

Continue to do what God says to do. Again, obedience is the key. It unlocks all the locks that were intended to block. It destroys all decoys. It gives you permission to enter into promotions, promises, peace, and prosperity. It's all prepared, and preserved for us. Receiving it all is a must. I receive. Will you receive with me?

First you must understand the following:

1. **It is impossible to buy a free gift.** Salvation is given to us freely by God's grace, and that is the way we have to live — by grace. God gives us forgiveness and grace daily, we just have to believe and receive.

2. **You are sin-free.** When God forgives your sins, He forgives all of your sins — past, present and future. You don't have to worry that you will keep sinning on purpose. If you are truly a believer and have a real relationship with God there is a new nature inside you. *"If any person is [ingrafted] in Christ (the Messiah) he is a new creation (a new creature altogether); the old [previous moral and spiritual condition] has passed away. Behold, the fresh and new has come!"* — 2 Corinthians 5:17 AMP

3. **You are changed by grace.** God doesn't expect you to change on your own. He is the source that gives us the grace and strength we need to change and do what's right.

4. **You hear God's word and are convinced by it.** The Word shows us who we are and reveals our sins. We have to realize what we're doing wrong before we can know what needs to be changed.

5. **Repent your sins.** Being repentant means you're truly sorry and will turn away from sin in the future.

6. **Study the Word.** Find the scriptures that deal with the sins you are trying to avoid, then use them like medicine and take them into your heart.

7. **Receive all God has for you.** Make the decision to believe in Him and His Word and you will receive God's' blessings and enjoy every day of your life. Use the bible as your instruction manual and learn how to grow into the new nature He has given you so you can become who He wants you to be.

"For it is by free grace (God's unmerited favor) that you are saved ... through [your] faith. And this [salvation] is not of yourselves [of your own doing, it came not through your own striving], but it is the gift of God; not because of works ... lest any man should boast. [It is not the result of what anyone can possibly do, so no one can pride himself in it or take glory to himself.]"

EPHESIANS 2:8-9 AMP

Grace and Favor Tours

God has sent me on these Grace and Favor tours to tell my testimony of what I went through before, during, and after Hurricane Harvey. This is the platform He's placed me on, for the body of Christ, and the world to see Him in a different light. He's showing off in and through me.

I have purpose in my heart to live by the cross. I continue to obey Him, and I keep receiving all these blessings He's getting through and to me.

Apostle Leroy Thompson spoke these words, and I believed and received them. He said, "Our seeing, hearing, and understanding must be in line with God." I stand firm on what he said. I'm obeying God's word. I'm succeeding because I believe and trust what His word says in this scripture.

> *So they got up early in the morning and went out into the Wilderness of Tekoa; and as they went out, Jehoshaphat stood and said, "Hear me, O Judah, and you inhabitants of Jerusalem! Believe and trust in the LORD your God and you will be established (secure). Believe and trust in His prophets and succeed.*
>
> 2 CHRONICLES 20:20 AMP

I will tell my testimony and people will hear, listen, and do what God says to do. I will give the people inspiration, impartation, information, and instructions from the words that I speak from God, by way of His Holy Spirit. People will listen because they want to learn how to handle difficult and disturbing distractions in their lives. They will want to know how to overcome these tests, trials, temptations, and turbulent times.

After explaining to them about what I went through, they will understand that these things are just temporary afflictions, and your moment will be what you make it to be. I will teach them how to be victors and not victims in this Water Breaking Faith.

Tests and trials come to show you what you need to do in order to obey God in every way. People will learn precepts and practices in order to receive the promotions and promises that have already been prepared and preserved for them.

Our prosperity pleases our Almighty God! My testimony will be heard across this world, even in foreign countries. One moment of favor is well worth a lifetime of labor. God will get His word out through me. I will allow Him to keep speaking to and through me by way of His Holy Spirit. This is key.

I shall always pray in the spirit and allow the tongues to flow. This allows us to go and grow in grace. We shall receive God's favor everywhere we go. We shall develop in the word of God. We will dominate, and live in dominion. Nothing will or can stop us as long as we continue to obey what He's said and will keep saying to and through us.

We will have what we say. Good or bad. Remember to speak what we want and not what we don't want. God gives us what we say.

Do you trust God to get you through the trying times? Here is some insight to letting God help you through the rough patches in your life:

1. Choose what to savor in life. By this, I mean don't dwell on the bad things in life — you're crippling your ability to trust God by doing this.

2. Don't get lost in sorrow and don't keep feeling sorry for yourself. When we allow those thoughts to dominate us, we create an atmosphere in our minds that makes it difficult to have faith in God. You don't want to wander the future without God because you've stopped trusting Him!

3. Discover joy. Slow down and spend some quiet time savoring the good in your life. Allow God to replenish your soul with the reminders of the little beauties that happen in the world. These

are priceless gifts from God, and they nourish us and give us hope in even the most difficult times.

4. Release your fears and give them to God. Savor God's replenishing promises. Do not let fear creep into your life. Once you've acknowledged and released the fear and you have a clean slate, be sure you regularly turn your thoughts to things that are true, honorable, right, pure, lovely, admirable, excellent and worthy of praise.

> [6]*Do not be anxious or worried about anything, but in everything [every circumstance and situation] by prayer and petition with thanksgiving, continue to make your [specific] requests known to God. 7 And the peace of God [that peace which reassures the heart, that peace] which transcends all understanding, [that peace which] stands guard over your hearts and your minds in Christ Jesus [is yours].*
>
> [8]*Finally, [a]believers, whatever is true, whatever is honorable and worthy of respect, whatever is right and confirmed by God's word, whatever is pure and wholesome, whatever is lovely and brings peace, whatever is admirable and of good repute; if there is any excellence, if there is anything worthy of praise, think continually on these things [center your mind on them, and implant them in your heart]. 9 The things which you have learned and received and heard and seen in me, practice these things [in daily life], and the God [who is the source] of peace and well-being will be with you.*
>
> PHILIPPIANS 4:6-9

Enjoy these GFITS

Getting
Fit
In
The
Spirit

1. Three-day supernatural cleansing from Holy Spirit.
2. Getting up early mornings, praying in the spirit daily, while dancing in the spirit.
3. Listening to worship songs from
4. Tasha Cobbs Lenard. You Know My Name
5. Maranda Curtis Open Heaven
6. CeCe Winans Bow Down
7. Dance until Holy Ghost say stop, and this is when God wants you to listen as He speaks revelations through you by way of His Holy Spirit.
8. Everything starts with you first, then you can help others. In helping others you must love yourself first, and then you can love others and help them catch on GFITS and receive all that God wants us to be, and become. Live in wealth and health.

"Beloved, I pray that in every way you may succeed and prosper and be in good health [physically], just as [I know] your soul prospers [spiritually]."

3 JOHN 1:2 AMP

"Love bears all things [regardless of what comes], believes all things [looking for the best in each one], hopes all things [remaining steadfast during difficult times], endures all things [without weakening]."

1 CORINTHIANS 13:7 AMP

Our Enemies are Revealed

Some enemies are hiding behind us, trying to sneak up on us. Call them out. Ask for help and it will come immediately. They will be eliminated. Other enemies can be sitting right in front of you. Called him out too and he will be banished.

Show the enemy you are not afraid of him and you will have power over him. He knows you have the help of the Holy Ghost and angels. When unlimited protection angels are always watching over you, nothing can harm you.

When you're a Christian, the enemy and his imps can't survived in your presence when you're covered by the blood of Jesus. Trinity is always with you to help you in every area of your life. You're never alone. When you call out for help, it's always available.

All help comes from Thee! The one and only true and living God!

We must recognize the enemy and he should know who we are. He must see the blood of Jesus on us and pass by our house. We have to call and cast him out; not try to pray him away, because he will stay. Demons drown when God is around, because He's alive in us.

Never trust the enemy. He sneaks and prowls around trying to see who he can destroy. Don't let him become a decoy. Don't let him punk or poison you.

Always be in a place to hear, see, listen and do what God says. You must have wisdom, knowledge, and understanding of His will for your life. The enemy won't be able to trick or trap you if you live in righteousness and obedience to God.

The enemy has deceived many, but he won't deceive you if you walk in His divinity — God the father, God the son, and God the Holy Spirit.

Do you feel the enemy working in your life? Here are a few signs to watch out for both in your life and in the church and how to battle them:

1. **Division.** This is one strategy the devil loves to use. He wants to create division in the church and in God's believers. This can come in the form of hatred, discord, jealousy, rage, dissension, envy, and conceit to mention a few.

2. **Arrogance (pride).** The most difficult test of character is success, because it makes it difficult to be humble. It's a big mistake to take credit when things are going well. Only God can claim that credit. Knowledge can also make you arrogant. Remember, as Paul says, knowledge puffs up; love builds up.

3. **Discouragement.** Do not fall into the trap of thinking you're no good, not making a difference, you're always making mistakes, etc. None of this is from God. The best antidote to a lie (all this discouragement) is the truth, so ground yourself in God's truth.

4. **Self-pity.** This is discouragement on steroids and sets in stone the seeds of thoughts discouragement sows. Self-pity can move you to the sidelines and is completely counter to the gospel. It allows satan to rob you of all joy, which delights him.

5. **Crossing moral lines.** Don't compromise, even on the small things. Once you start down that path, it's easy to make bigger and bigger compromises. If you're not faithful in the little things, you won't be faithful in the bigger ones.

Watching out for these things and knowing they could happen is half the battle. If you don't recognize the enemy's strategies, it's hard to defeat them. Stay vigilant and the enemy can never win.

When God Speaks, Everyone and Every Thing Listens

It's in the shout. All spiritual blessings will come about. Open your mouth. God wants you out. Holy Ghost filled, will reveal. This is the only way for the secrets to come out today. They are hidden from the enemy. He doesn't understand the tongues. You've won.

The praises have begun. Worship Him in spirit and in truth. This is what God wants you to do. Whatever you're facing has a name. God's name is above every name. Call out His name over the name that's got you down or bound. Jesus! Jesus! Jesus!

The blood will get you out of the flood — whatever is flooding your life that you couldn't control. The water came and you'll be rescued in Jesus' name. The rescuers will come because you call on Him ahead of time. You shine all the time in His Divine light.

God says, "Walk in line, You are mine."

I know that God was, He is, and He's still around. God says, "Even when you can't see Me, I'm there. Even when you can't feel Me, I'm there. In the morning when you awake and arise, I'm there. It's Me that's standing there, saying get up. Even when things might get rough, I make them right. Keep loving Me with all your might. Keep Me in your sight — your sight that only you can see — it's Me standing before thee. Your feeling that only you can feel — I'm real. I'm there. I'm everywhere. Everywhere there is. I'm in the field. I've been revealed. When you were healed. I'm there. I care.

Do you care? This is the question because you sometimes act as though you don't. Know that I am in your wants. Desires are to inspire, now inquire. You are being used, don't be confused. The things you've been experiencing are not a coincidence. There's no coincidence in Me. I know all, and see all. I'm everywhere at all times.

I only come when you ask Me. Invitation is your nature. You should always invite Me in if you want to win. Daily communication is your nature. Never go a day without communicating with Me and having Me in your conversations.

I'm the glory in your story. Testimony. You've been through the test. Now I'm on it. Whatever your *it* is. Increase Treasure. I've preserved and watched over it.

Nothing and no one can sneak in and snatch what you've been set apart to receive. Believe and receive. You've been blessed indeed. It's all about Me! I am that I am has spoken! Love and live life knowing that the enemy's curses have already been broken.

How do you share your Christian testimony? Here are some tips to help you get the Word out:

1. Don't try to copy what others do. No two testimonies are alike — we're all individuals. God will use your unique experience to help you speak to others.

2. Be authentic. If you try to be someone you're not, you're not being true to your Christian beliefs.

3. Tell your before and after story. Talk about the way your life was before being saved and then highlight how it has changed after.

4. Avoid cliches and Christian "jargon." Filling your conversations with lots of biblical phrases and words won't be meaningful to unbelievers. Speak in plain English so everyone will understand what you're trying to say.

5. Keep your testimony warm and personal. Don't get preachy or accusatory. You are not there to judge. Be sure you make your story personal by saying I and me.

6. Keep it short. You want to make people curious to know more, not bore them with a lengthy talk.

TMI

Thinking
Mediating
Information

What thoughts are we allowing to park inside our minds? Whatever we concentrate on the most that's what we see and even start believing. So a man thinks in his heart, so he is.

You have what you say. What do you want to come your way? Numbers 14:28 says, "God gives you the very things He hears you say." Think big, dream big! Mediate on what you want and see yourself there on the canvas of your imagination!

Information that's received in your mind is what you believe will happen for or to you!

Think on the good things, and see yourself there before you get there. When you start receiving, you relate to those things because you've been there before.

Have you ever seen something and thought, I've been here before? When I came through the flood, I knew I would make it out, but I didn't know how. When I lost everything, I knew I would get it all back and more, but I didn't know how at that time. I'm letting you know you can survive your hurricane and thrive. If the water hadn't of broken, my testimony couldn't have been spoken.

When you are walking along side of your different situations and you don't know what to do or how to do it, Holy Spirit leads you into your now. Any bad or trying situation, Holy Spirit helps you and turns them into a wow!

You see physical fire; however, it's not physical, it's having faith in the purification. You're going through the process to receive the promises that have already been prepared and preserved for you. You've been tested, tried, and purified.

God lays out His word right in front, side and all around you. It's your job to sit down on the right side of Him, not the wrong side, which is the enemy's side. We have to choose His word, read it, receive it, and obey it. In His word there's a wealth of information to help us through any given situation.

We continue seeing and know that we are safe, and seated with Christ Jesus. There's no other way than to follow His directions every day. Keep hearing what He has to say. Obey, and we will never go astray.

Follow Holy Spirit's leadership; He will always show us the way. We must stay in line and shine in His Divine light all the time. His Divinity is the Trinity!

When we go through and come out the other side, God allows us to look as though we never went through the trial.

Receive everything now, that God has spoken! You've been tried and tested, now receive your blessings!

Let Praises Rise

All I want is for you is to be gloried; you to be lifted high

We are under an open heaven. Receiving from the Courts of Heaven. The verdict is in. I win. Judge God has given us everything we've asked for according to His word. Our requests have been heard. I receive.

Build up His kingdom now. The blessings shall continue to come about — never stopping, a continual flow. How and where we don't need to know.

Continue to flow, feed, and lead. You are blessed indeed. You have no needs. They've already been met. Your blessings have broken the net. Net breaking blessings.

You ain't seen nothing yet. Miracles, signs, and wonders — that's you. Continue to do what He says to do.

New doors have been opened. The land is green. The blessings are here. The nations have come to me. They receive answers from Him, through me, by way of Holy Ghost. I'm shinning like a house on the hill, and through me, God's Glory is revealed.

I am in favor. I'm walking in abundance and obeying everything from the Holy Ghost. I've taken over everywhere I go, and everywhere I am. It's in God plans. He's given me the lands.

Plenty, plenty, it's for many. It's my make-up. I receive all the beautiful things He's made me to be. This beauty that's in the eye of the beholder. If you behold the look, that's what you receive. Look into and on the inside of where God abides, where satan can't survive or hide.

I'm hidden under God's Almighty wings. I've been released for all the world to see. I'm the light that shines bright. In His Divine, I'm always on His mind, and He's on mine.

Another love I will never find. Loving God is what I continue to do. Giving Him the glory and seeing all these wonderful blessings keep coming through. What He's done for me He will do the same for you.

I keep worshipping and praising God from the inside and He continues to abide. In His will that's where I continue to reside. Glory hallelujah! This is the word from God that He's given to you! Receive! I receive!

Eight Things that Come When You're Obeying the Will of God

Your seeing, hearing and understanding must be in line with Him.

1. Truth...Freedom John 8:32 AMP
2. Trust...Focus Proverbs 3:5
3. Transition...From 2 Corinthians 5:17 old man to new man
4. Traditions...Facts Colossians 2:8 instead of knowing truth
5. Transformation...Form 2 Timothy 3:5 of Godliness
6. Transference...Filled Acts 2:4 with His Spirit
7. Triumphing...Flowing 1 Corinthians 2:9 eyes haven't seen
8. Trinity...Faith in God totally relying on, believing, trusting, and obeying Him for all things that He's given us by grace through faith. Knowing the way has been made.

When we know the truth, we can have freedom from the hands of the enemy. We must totally obey and trust in God so our focus shall be on Him only. It's a must that we transition from the old and allow all things to become new and be renewed, reborn, and spiritually transformed, as we become new creatures created in Christ Jesus.

Never be caught up in the tradition and facts of this empty, deceptive world. Don't follow people just because they sound intelligent. We must continually walk in the truths of God, the teachings of Christ Jesus and the cross, and his resurrection.

Know that we've received transformation and we don't just have a form of godliness or religion. Don't deny the power of God, because this cancels your faith.

Since you've been transformed, keep yourself centered around like-minded people who are living in the will of God and people who have set their affections on things above and serving Jesus.

We have the transference of God's Spirit as we've been filled with His Holy Spirit. Since we are filled, we can continue triumphing and flowing in the things which our eyes have not seen and our ears have not heard, and which have not entered the heart of man. All that God has prepared for those who love Him is ours.

Obey Him and gratefully recognize the benefits of the blessings He's given us. In having the Trinity operating in our lives, we must have faith in God, which is totally relying on, believing, trusting, and obeying Him for all things that He's given us by grace through faith. Know the way has been made.

God's Servant

God made me a sign and a wonder.
I'm sent to do His will.
I'm saturated in His glory; soaked in the blood of His son Jesus.
I'm settled here without fear, obeying His Holy Spirit and
living under an open heaven.
I receive His promises, provisions, promotions and promises.
Amen

You love from heaven above. You are harmless as doves. God says, "love is key to receive from Me." Sharing is caring and you are doing this because you love and care about the people you are sharing with.

You are releasing blessings for them when you speak God's word out of your mouth. You shout because you have been brought out. You are restored, renewed, and rendering services to Almighty God. That's what we're called to do.

Know that it's not always about you. Outpouring, overflowing, and outstanding outcomes have begun in your ministry, all because you kept the faith to the finish. You always allowed God to be in it. You accepted the call, run the play, just obey.

Remain, remember, retain, and always do everything in Jesus' name.

Your life has been refreshed and Jesus' blood has removed all the mess. You've passed the tests. Now you shall always live to give, forgive, and know you have been made from God's best.

"For we are His workmanship [His own master work, a work of art], created in Christ Jesus [reborn from above—spiritually transformed,

renewed, ready to be used] for good works, which God prepared [for us] beforehand [taking paths which He set], so that we would walk in them [living the good life which He prearranged and made ready for us]."

EPHESIANS 2:10 AMP

Using God's tools you will never loose. Now that you've put them on, don't take them off. Never stop moving, unless He says stand still. Your purpose is to always be in His will. The fight was finished on the cross because Jesus paid the cost.

Shut the door on satan and his imps. The enemy tries to sift you as wheat, and keep you at his feet.

God has come so that you might have life and have it more abundantly. You have been given all sufficiency. Right now, you see some lack; however, know that you are still on track.

Know that everything has been restored, reserved, and you must receive it all. When God makes your reservation, you must show up. Cancellation is not an option. Check in and see what's been placed in your room.

Peace, and pleasure, is in the place you're positioned in. There's no bed of affliction in this room. No doom and gloom in this room. No depression, no darkness, no devastation, no distraction, and no destruction, in this room. What God has placed in this room is far greater than what the enemy tried and kept trying to put there.

God allows His Holy Spirit to work for you and through you, always getting things to you, as long as you continue to obey Him, and never the enemy.

Rejoice and be exceedingly glad!

Be sure to exhibit the characteristics of a good Christian servant, including:

1. **Be a follower *and* a leader.** A faithful Christian servant loves the Heavenly Father and follows Jesus. This means that when he makes choices in his life, he chooses what Jesus would choose and goes where Jesus would go. A faithful servant is available to teach others how to follow Jesus too. *"If anyone serves Me, he*

must [continue to faithfully] follow Me [without hesitation, holding steadfastly to Me, conforming to My example in living and, if need be, suffering or perhaps dying because of faith in Me]; and wherever I am [in heaven's glory], there will My servant be also. If anyone serves Me, the Father will honor him." — John 12:26 AMP

2. **Be Humble.** A faithful servant does not act superior or better than others. He is humble, not proud. He remembers why Jesus came to earth — to humbly give His life for all.

3. **Be Meek.** Being meek is not being weak. Being meek is exhibiting controlled strength. A good servant knows when it is necessary to be meek and serve in a way that displays this Christ-like characteristic.

4. **Be Patient and restrained.** Be careful not to impose your calling onto others. You cannot make someone volunteer or serve. Do not force someone to serve in a capacity they were not called to do. When we do this, we're putting them in a position that does not glorify God.

5. **Share your gifts.** A good Christian servant must give at the offering plate and also be willing to give of his gifts and talents. Doing this shows your commitment to serve others. It shows that we serve out of a heart of gratitude for the gifts we've been given.

6. **Share your experience.** Learn from and share your experience with others so they may see that with patience comes experience. Also know that experience produces hope. Sometimes people in hopeless situations just need to be served.

7. **Be selfless.** Do not put your needs before others' needs. Jesus was selfless and came to serve, not be served. He made the ultimate sacrifice, and like him, we should serve without concern for our needs. *"Do nothing from selfishness or empty conceit [through factional motives, or strife], but with [an attitude of] humility [being neither arrogant nor self-righteous], regard others as more important than yourselves. 4 Do not merely look out for your own personal interests, but also for the interests of others."* — Philippians 2:3-4

God's Gift of Life

Greatness comes from God's gift of grace, through His Glory. This is the light that shines through His son Jesus. This is the light that He's given us. This light that shines, because He's always on our minds. There's no other love that we will be able to find. Thank You, Lord, for this gift. I'm grateful!

I worship You in spirit and in truth. I obey You. You are the lover of my life. Thank you for giving us Your son, Jesus Christ, as our living sacrifice.

I never have to think twice. Your thoughts are my thoughts. Holy Ghost thinks through my mind all the time. Angels bring God's gifts on the scene. Now, they can be seen. What an amazing thing.

I'm living in God's plans. I lift up my hands. I raise up and reach out and receive everything He's given me. I am awake to God's presence — I no longer sleep. I've raised up, and I'm on my feet.

I've chosen to sit at His feet. From His table I eat. There can't be anything else put before me. I'm no longer asleep and I see the enemy's schemes. I've allowed God's voice to be heard, even when I was sleeping.

Holy Ghost is my helper. God is my life line. This line that I've grabbed a-hold of and I won't let go. There's no kinks or knots in this line. It can't be redirected. This line stretches long and far.

This is the path that I follow. I never let go or get out of line. I've chosen to hold on tight, and I won't let anything make me lose sight. The path is clear. I have no fear. Faith is the only way.

I continue to hear, listen, and do. His voice I continue to hear. Even though I was sleep, and my eyes were closed, His voice I know. I've found and chosen to follow the light, even in the darkness. I will allow the light to override and outshine any darkness. Darkness, that I once turned on the light to see in. Darkness was from the enemy, but I didn't have a clue.

Now I'm awake, and I know what to do. I follow through. Never getting stuck while going through. My outcome is what God has given, and I've allowed it all to line up with His desires for me.

I keep receiving. I'm never deceived. I have dominion. I am continuing to be grateful for the gifts, the glory, and the light. This is the only pathway. Thank You, Lord!

Are you fighting the darkness? Here are some tips that may help you:

1. **Bring what you need to light the lamp.** Sometimes you have to do the work to light the lamps, just like the Israelites did when God commanded them to light the lamps.

2. **Turn your eyes heavenward.** Meeting God's gaze can be spiritually and emotionally healing. True, deep spiritual healing can only be found if you meet with God, rest in Jesus and invite Holy Spirit to refresh and revive your soul.

3. **Tend your faith.** Trust God to keep loving, blessing and embracing you. As long as you tend your faith, He will always be there for you.

4. **Keep your faith constantly.** Make yourself a shining symbol of God's blessings, warmth, comfort and connection with God.

You're Surrounded by His glory!

Appreciated
Approvals
Awards
Actions

You are surrounded by God's glory! Mighty moves in the spirit have come, because you allow My will to be done. Your natural has become the supernatural. All needs have been met.

Desires, and dominion you have. You keep subduing, replenishing, and multiplying in these mighty moves from Me. You are released from lack and into all manifested abundance. Abundance shall keep moving into your hands. It's in My plans.

These plans prosper you, and you have the expected end. This prosperity is from Me, because you have continued to walk in My obedience. I've allowed you to be appreciated for what you've done. You are recognized by all, even those who weren't on the receiving end of what you did.

People have heard and will continue to hear about the words that you've spoken from Me, through all forms of communication. Your preaching and teaching has gone to a new level in Christ Jesus. You have been approved. People will do what you want them to do. Everything obeys you. Call what you want to come. It's done.

Your actions are key. Keep sowing your seeds that have been ministered from Me. You are blessed indeed. Your abundance has increased supernaturally! One lump sum has come! Manifested abundance has been released to you! It has already been moved in to your hands. Quickly, suddenly, and soon you will see, all because you continue to believe Me.

You've been set apart — sanctified and made holy. This is what people know about you. You've been through the fiery furnace and come through without the smell of smoke, all because of what God has spoken.

All these blessings will keep coming. Stay focused and in faith. Keep reaping and receiving. Remember Apostle Thompson spoke these words, "You have a receiving anointing."

Always remember those that paved the way for you. Those that were there, but didn't do for you, you can't give credit to, just recognize their presence with you.

Keep moving in My Divine light. Always shine. Keep loving Me all the time. You've made up your mind. Don't allow anything to get you out of line. I am the almighty God! Receive and enjoy!

> [17][I always pray] that the God of our Lord Jesus Christ, the Father of glory, may grant you a spirit of wisdom and of revelation [that gives you a deep and personal and intimate insight] into the true knowledge of Him [for we know the Father through the Son]. [18]And [I pray] that the eyes of your heart [the very center and core of your being] may be enlightened [flooded with light by the Holy Spirit], so that you will know and cherish the [a]hope [the divine guarantee, the confident expectation] to which He has called you, the riches of His glorious inheritance in the [b]saints (God's people), [19]and [so that you will begin to know] what the immeasurable and unlimited and surpassing greatness of His [active, spiritual] power is in us who believe. These are in accordance with the working of His mighty strength [20]which He [c]produced in Christ when He raised Him from the dead and seated Him at His own right hand in the heavenly places, [21]far above all rule and authority and power and dominion [whether angelic or human], and [far above] every name that is named [above every title that can be conferred], not only in this age and world but also in the one to come.
>
> EPHESIANS 1:17-21

Pray Without Ceasing

Questions I ask myself:
    Who's praying for you while you're praying for others?
    Who's pouring into you while you're pouring into others?
    Who's picking you up when you're picking up others?

Answers from God:
- Don't sabotage your thoughts by thinking things not from Me. Let your thoughts be of the mind of Christ.
- I'm your heavy load sharer, and I'm your burden barer.
- I'm your lifter when you are down, and I'm always around.
- I've prayed that your faith fail thee not.
- The cross took care of all your thoughts.
- Jesus paid the price and he was the living sacrifice.
- Because you are made in His image you sometimes sacrifice for others.
- Everything you thought you were not, know that I've poured out My spirit in you.
- Continue to pray without ceasing.
- Know that because of your prayers, things happen.
- The effectual, fervent prayers of the righteous availeth much.
- Don't let nothing stop you, even when thing get tough.
- I made you, and you are My diamond in the rough.
- You've been smoothed out, and things from satan slide off.
- Know that you have a Capitol of states, however My Courts of Heaven is the Capitol of all states.

You are living under an open heaven, and your state of being is always existing through the mind of Christ Jesus.

I've made you live in Christ Jesus.

Receive.

Thank you Lord I receive!

Appreciate the Gift

*Jesus Christ laid down his life so that we might live.
Living is our choice. Just obey God's voice.*

Don't live life like it's business as usual. Appreciate the gift you've been given. Don't allow the gift to sit unopened, unused, or unappreciated. The gift has been given to live in righteousness. We must not live in fornication, adultery, lack, disobedience, or anything else that causes us to live outside of God's will.

Jesus was given to us as a gift from God. He sacrificed. He paid the price for us to live right. Never take that for granted.

We have dominion. We have been made to be fruitful, multiply, subdue, and replenish. We must not let our lives be depleted, and we must know that the gift is needed.

The enemy seeks and sees who he can destroy, so he can cause their spiritual death. Stop him from doing his job.

Some people are living life without appreciating God-given and living sacrifice. Some people don't want the gift. They've just laid it down unopened and don't even think about it until things get bad or they're afraid.

Some use the gift temporarily, and some even throw it in the trash and never retrieve it. They just leave it. Some don't know the purpose and plan for the gift. If you never open the gift, you won't know its purpose or even what it is.

If the gift isn't used properly, you miss the treasure, teaching, training, trusting, and triumph in it. Know that the gift is for those who want it and are willing and obedient enough to receive it and use it the way it was meant to be used.

The gift is love. The gift was given out of love. The gift was given for us to love. The gift was given to get love through and to us.

For God so [greatly] loved and dearly prized the world, that He [even] gave His [One and] only begotten Son, so that whoever believes and trusts in Him [as Savior]
shall not perish, but have eternal life.

JOHN 3:16 AMP

Use the gift in wisdom, which is the right way, according to the will and word of God. If you do this, you will excel and go far.

Use the name of Jesus, right where you are. The name of Jesus causes you to be set apart. The name of Jesus is our strong tower. Use the name of Jesus every hour. Know that you have authority, and have been given power. The name of Jesus has been freely given. Accept and receive him, and know that you've been forgiven. This is why you're living. Live. Forgive. Live in righteousness. Obey God and receive His gift.

[8]For it is by grace [God's remarkable compassion and favor drawing you to Christ] that you have been saved [actually delivered from judgment and given eternal life] through faith. And this [salvation] is not of yourselves [not through your own effort], but it is the [undeserved, gracious] gift of God; [9]not as a result of [your] works [nor your attempts to keep the Law], so that no one will [be able to] boast or take credit in any way [for his salvation].

EPHESIANS 2:8

Wake Up, Receive Your Stuff

Supernatural
Transference
Unlimited
Fruit
Finances

Why are you trying to sleep when God wants to speak? God says, rising early is key to hear from Me. When you want to sleep long, it's not wrong, however when someone else calls you answer the phone. Get out the bed. Right now, get sleep out of your head. Get out of the gate don't be late. Love and not hate. It's all for Christ's sake.

Love for Him makes you love them. Be careful not to say things you don't mean. Make sure we don't cancel our dreams. God's love is real. Don't be so caught up in how you feel. Most importantly be filled with Holy Spirit, He's for real.

Well, some people say you can't believe in something you can't see or feel. I say, allowing Holy Spirit to lead and guide you will take you out of your natural comfort zone and bring you into things God wants you to own.

Keep cover. Don't uncover what God has allowed to be covered. Never go back and redo what He's allowed to be done. Your life in Christ Jesus has been made over. Again, keep cover. You will soon be discovered. People have been searching for you and they don't even know why.

God has allowed them to give to you in supernatural supply. You are within reach, and you reach, because My word you continue to teach and preach. You aren't putting on a show. You shall grow now, as I show you how.

Keep listening in, and you'll always win. Keep praising, even when it seems crazy. I've turned your negatives into positives.

Don't think it strange when people come to you in My name. You will know because it'll show in the growth. Continue to go, even when it doesn't look like you growing. People are listening to you, and they will soon come to you when they are ready and want to.

They have been set free, but they are still asking if it's from Me? Soon you will see. My Kingdom shall be filled. It's in My will.

You will have all sufficiency and more than enough. It has come, even though it's been rough. You are tough and built to last. You've been brought out from the past and the last. Now you are first, because you've quenched your spiritual thirst and you've come out of the trench.

You've awakened from your sleep. Again, never sleep when I want to speak. Receive all this prosperity! Know that it's from Me! It's your choice, choose to rejoice! Enjoy! This word is from almighty God!

Continual Worship!

Release unlimited and lifetime of blessings and increase!

When you worship God in spirit and in truth, lift your hands high, saying, "God do what you want to do through me!" When you worship God, you're born again from above. You're spiritually transformed, renewed, and set apart for His purpose.

While you're worshipping, I remove everything not like Him, and I replace it with His glory. Take your place and position yourself in being proud to worship God in spirit and in truth. Exalt and lift up Jesus Christ, and do not worship yourself or man. Say, "God allow Your glory to be revealed through me."

"for we [who are born-again have been reborn from above—spiritually transformed, renewed, set apart for His purpose and] are the true circumcision, who worship in the Spirit of God and glory and take pride and exult in Christ Jesus and place no confidence [in what we have or who we are] in the flesh—"

PHILIPPIANS 3:3 AMP

When you worship, allow Holy Spirit to help, as He leads and guides you into the Holy of Holies and the presence of God. Worship and praise God gives us favor with all people, and He adds to His church daily those who were being saved.

Dance in His presence. Worship God in your sowing, and grow in grace, gifts, and goodness. He's pleased to prosper you. Thank Him for allowing you to succeed.

> "By this the Holy Spirit signifies that the way into the Holy Place [the true Holy of Holies and the presence of God] has not yet been disclosed as long as the first or outer tabernacle is still standing [that is, as long as the Levitical system of worship remains a recognized institution],"
>
> HEBREWS 9:8 AMP

> "Day after day they met in the temple [area] continuing with one mind, and breaking bread in various private homes. They were eating their meals together with joy and generous hearts, praising God continually, and having favor with all the people. And the Lord kept adding to their number daily those who were being saved."
>
> ACTS 2:46-47 AMP

When you worship, ask God to teach you how to live in His truth, and to direct your heart with inspired reverence. Submit to God's wonders and delight in continual righteousness. Be determined to live a godly life in Christ Jesus."

> "Teach me Your way, O LORD, I will walk and live in Your truth; Direct my heart to fear Your name [with awe-inspired reverence and submissive wonder]."
>
> PSALMS 86:11 AMP

With Jesus in your life, you are never alone. He will take your hands, and move you out of any battles, while He fights them for you. He will take you out of the battle of sickness and disease. Yes, that's what He'll do for you.

Rest, Jesus, Rest

We must say, "Rest, Jesus, rest," and then say, "Yes, Jesus, yes." Can Jesus rest comfortably in you? Can Jesus do what He wants through you, for you, and to you? We are made in Christ Jesus. Therefore, as Jesus is, so are we.

Because of the blood of Jesus nothing can stop us or destroy us. The blood of Jesus rests in us. Saying yes to Him is a must. If we trust Him, we know the truth and it makes us free and we receive our increase.

Our growth is in Christ Jesus. When we grow in Christ, we help others to grow too, because of His sacrifice.

God says, "Choose whom you will serve — self, satan, or the Savior?"

I say rest, Jesus, please, rest in me. I receive Him resting in me. Again, let Him rest comfortably. Don't allow His rest to be disturbed.

Now that you've heard. Believe, and you shall receive. The word of His prophet brings prosperity. He's pleased, and you shall succeed.

Large abundance has come to us today! I receive. Will you believe and receive?

When Jesus rests freely in you, situations and circumstances not of God have to flee. Everything not of God cannot stay with you. You must call it out, cast it out, cancel it, and curse it from the root.

Lack and limitations, and depression and oppression are gone. Yes — rest, Jesus, rest. Souls are saved, when you allow Jesus to rest in you every day. Satan can't stay or come in when you allow Jesus to rest within you. The blood of Jesus blocks it.

When Jesus rests in you, the blood of Jesus resides in you. You know what to do. Let him work through and for you. Allow all of God's promises to get to you. When Jesus rests in you, Holy Spirit leads and guides you. Work is done through you. When Jesus rests in you, we are His workmanship, and created in Him.

> *"For we are His workmanship [His own master work, a work of art], created in Christ Jesus [reborn from above—spiritually transformed, renewed, ready to be used] for good works, which God prepared [for us] beforehand [taking paths which He set], so that we would walk in them [living the good life which He prearranged and made ready for us]."*
>
> EPHESIANS 2:10 AMP

When Jesus rests in us, we can do more than we could have ever imagined.

> *"Now to Him who is able to [carry out His purpose and] do super abundantly more than all that we dare ask or think [infinitely beyond our greatest prayers, hopes, or dreams], according to His power that is at work within us,"*
>
> EPHESIANS 3:20 AMP

Yes — rest, Jesus, rest. When He rests in us, we are crucified with Him. He lives in us, and we no longer have to live in the flesh, but by faith in Him because He loved us so much that He died for our sins, and rose back up again.

> *"I have been crucified with Christ [that is, in Him I have shared His crucifixion]; it is no longer I who live, but Christ lives in me. The life I now live in the body I live by faith [by adhering to, relying on, and completely trusting] in the Son of God, who loved me and gave Himself up for me."*
>
> GALATIANS 2:20 AMP

In the Name of Our Savior Jesus Christ

Seek and serve the sovereign and supernatural God, all in the name of our Savior Jesus Christ, our living sacrifice. Never think twice. For you, He gave up His life. See what's about to come to you.

Obedient is what we must be. It should never be an option. Choose God and never loose. Choose the enemy and he will bury you. Your hearing and doing is how to follow and move forward and not backward when serving God.

"Then the master told the servant, 'Go out into the highways and along the hedges, and compel them to come in, so that my house may be filled [with guests].'"

LUKE 14:23 AMP

Reflecting on God

As I sit back and reflect on God, He reminds me that's He's the real redeemer. He's called me to live a righteous life. He's restored my soul and always leads me in the way that I must go. I've been moved to the place and position where I now know that He's my everything, and I'm hidden under His almighty wings.

I have received all of His promises by grace through faith. I know they have come to me today. I always expect to live in this large place, this place of plenty where more is coming each day. His word I continue to obey.

He's given me His son, Jesus Christ, as a living sacrifice. I know he lives in me, and I don't have to think twice. I thank God for Jesus giving up His life, and rising back up again just to cleanse me of my sins.

We must live in the now and realize God has made us an open show. All the world will see what He's made us to be. We've been made alive in Jesus Christ. When we allow him to rest, rule, reign, and remain in us, we can't be destroyed. We have dominion over all things, even the devil and his decoys.

We are exceedingly glad. We have more peace than we ever had, and we never have to be sad. We have clarity in our minds, as we keep shinning in His Divine light.

This is our time. We live in every season, for this very reason. God deserves our best. Because He is, I am. He is my life. I am living right. We are His called-out ones.

Holy is the way we must live. Don't hold on to things that we should have let go of. Forgive. Know that when we pray, our prayers won't be effective if we hold onto the things that could cause us to be redirected.

> *"Whenever you stand praying, if you have anything against anyone, forgive him [drop the issue, let it go], so that your Father who is in heaven will also forgive you your transgressions and wrongdoings [against Him and others]. [But if you do not forgive, neither will your Father in heaven forgive your transgressions."]"*
>
> MARK 11:25-26 AMP

> *"Pay attention and always be on guard [looking out for one another]! If your brother sins and disregards God's precepts, solemnly warn him; and if he repents and changes, forgive him."*
>
> LUKE 17:3 AMP

Living in Christ Jesus, we stay in line with our design. We are made in His image. No other design fits the one that was made especially for you. God has picked the pattern for you. Let it do what it needs to do. It'll look well on you.

Keep the faith. Always do things God's way. Obey. Live according to His will. Speak what He speaks, and He'll cause things to obey what you say.

And the Lord said, "If you have [confident, abiding] faith in God [even as small] as a mustard seed, you could say to this mulberry tree [which has very strong roots], 'Be pulled up by the roots and be planted in the sea'; and [if the request was in agreement with the will of God] it would have obeyed you."

LUKE 17:6 AMP

"This is the [remarkable degree of] confidence which we [as believers are entitled to] have before Him: that if we ask anything according to His will, [that is, consistent with His plan and purpose] He hears us. And if we know [for a fact, as indeed we do] that He hears and listens to us in whatever we ask, we [also] know [with settled and absolute knowledge] that we have [granted to us] the requests which we have asked from Him."

1 JOHN 5:14-15 AMP

We must know that it's already done. Challenges comes to strengthen you and make you better than before. You have already been set in this large place. You don't have to try and be bigger, however just thrive to be better. Be the best and the better that you can be. Serve God wholeheartedly.

"But first and most importantly seek (aim at, strive after) His kingdom and His righteousness [His way of doing and being right—the attitude and character of God], and all these things will be given to you also."

MATTHEW 6:33 AMP

Release the Restraints

Be unrestrained by man. Unrestrained by the works of your own hands. Unrestrained by the enemy. After you've done all, just stand. Stand strong. This place from God is where you belong. You can't go wrong. It won't be long. God decrees all His blessings you will soon see. It's not just for me.

> *"Yes indeed, it won't be long now." GOD's Decree. "Things are going to happen so fast your head will swim, one thing fast on the heels of the other. You won't be able to keep up. Everything will be happening at once—and everywhere you look, blessings! Blessings like wine pouring off the mountains and hills. I'll make everything right again for my people Israel: "They'll rebuild their ruined cities. They'll plant vineyards and drink good wine. They'll work their gardens and eat fresh vegetables. And I'll plant them, plant them on their own land. They'll never again be uprooted from the land I've given them." GOD, your God, says so."*
>
> AMOS 9:13-15 MSG

Stop looking and listening to the wrong voice. Now, make the choice. Who will you serve? Don't worry about the wrong things. Know that God has already released the restraints and given you everything.

Obey Him when you hear, listen, do, and see. He's hearing and listening and will keep doing for you. You have to make sure you do for Him. Obey and serve, that's what He deserves. Your life He's preserved.

He's released you into His promises, and released you from the predators and predicaments of your past problems. Old things have passed away. Behold all things have become new and are new, just for you.

Take your place, keep your place, don't get out of place. God has given you this large place to rest, rule, reign, remain, and reside in. Be careful, courageous, confident, compassionate, and own where you belong. It won't be long!

> [1]"Now it shall be, if you diligently listen to and obey the voice of the Lord your God, being careful to do all of His commandments which I am commanding you today, the Lord your God will set you high above all the nations of the earth. [2]All these blessings will come upon you and overtake you if you pay attention to the voice of the Lord your God.
>
> DEUTERONOMY 28:1-2 AMP

Mighty Victorious Believers' Prayer

Father thank You for being my God, my lover, my comforter, my healer, my deliverer, and my strength. Thank You for allowing me to be sent, and not went. With Holy Spirit's help I will never go by myself.

Thank You for being my will in the middle of Your will. I praise You for being my Alpha and Omega. You are my beginning, my ending, and my all in-between.

Father, thank You for all Your promises that You've given me by grace through faith. Thank You, God, for not just making a way, but continuing to make a way, even when I couldn't see a way. I receive everything today, and I have just what I say, and I keep saying.

I choose to speak only what You speak, and what You have spoken. Thank You, Father, that I can never be broken. Nothing can stop me. I'll be walking and obeying Your will, that's already been done.

I've won because of Your son, Jesus Christ, our living sacrifice. He laid down His life. He paid the price. Now I can live and forgive.

Thank You, Father, for forgiving me for all my sins, and allowing me to win over and over again. I win every time, because I walk in Your Divine light — Your Trinity.

Thank You for Your host of unlimited, innumerable angels that are encamped all around and about me. I trust You. I shall continue to lean, and rely on You.

I say, "Holy Spirit, help me to keep obeying daily, in every way." I call only what You want to come. It's Your will being done.

I'm living under an open heaven. The valves are open. Everything flows, flourishes, and floods through Your channels. Father thank You for giving us control over the channels. We make our way prosperous and have good success.

Being Your children, You've made us far greater than the rest. We are Your very best. Fitly joined together. Thank You for Your workmanship, Your master work, Your work of art.

Father, thank You for creating me in Christ Jesus, allowing me to be reborn from above, spiritually transformed, renewed, and ready to be used for Your good works.

God, thank You for preparing me beforehand, and I now take paths which You set, and I walk in them.

Father, thank You for this good life that I'm living, which You prearranged and made ready for me.

Father God, thank You for our Apostle Leroy Thompson, and the royal family.

Live a Complete and Prosperous Life

THINGS THAT MUST BE DONE TO COMPLETELY DESTROY SATAN:

1. Call out evil.
2. Cast evil out of your life
3. Cancel negative thinking
4. Keep God in your heart and mind at all times

THINGS THAT MUST BE DONE TO LIVE A COMPLETE AND PROSPEROUS LIFE:

1. Be a Servant
2. Sowing seeds of the Word
3. Speak to others about Jesus
4. Live a Christian life

In the Courts of Heaven, I saw the light first, then there was a snake and then darkness. After the darkness disappeared, the light returned, and continued to remain. God showed me what the outcome would be before I saw the snake, which was the darkness of satan. He showed me that even though you might go through the dark situations that satan brings, you've already been made to come out as shining lights in the darkness of the world.

In order to completely destroyed satan, we must do the things listed above and they must be done by His body of baptized believers. There has to be the calling, casting, canceling out of satan at all times. Thank God for destroying him.

If we as believers desire to live a complete and prosperous life, we must possess particular characteristics, and live in obedience to God.

Our lights should be shining. We should be servants, sowing seed, speaking about Jesus, and living Christian lives. When we do this, we will receive Supernatural Surplus from God Himself. We will live sufficient lives in Christ Jesus.

We must never allow our light to be taken away by the darkness that we might face in this world. Even though the world was dark and void at first, God is so powerful and magnificent that He allowed His Spirit to present itself. He operated in the dark and void to make the light come through. He replaced the nothingness and emptiness of the world.

We have already received by grace through faith everything He wants to come our way. He's always with us in the dark situations and emptiness we might experience in life. He never leaves or forsakes us.

We have to be able to see, hear, listen, obey, and understand, what He's done, and know we've already won. Even though you go through bad times, it doesn't mean God's not with you.

Look at it this way. He was with the three Hebrew boys in the fiery furnace. He was with Daniel in the lion's den. He was with Moses leading the children through the Red Sea. These are all examples showing that He's always with us, no matter what.

When I go into the Courts of Heaven, God allows me to see what I see. My eyes are enlightened to see what He shows me. I trust Him, I believe and receive, then I can speak what His spirit has spoken to me.

My prayer for you is that you do as I do and allow God's spirit to speak to you. Obey what He says to do.

We are all His servants called out to serve Him and His Kingdom, which allows His will to be done. We must know that God gave us the most precious gift, Jesus Christ, His Son. Understand that the battles in life can't be over until we've won. We can't live prosperous lives until we believe the prophet. Let's keep following through, while obeying God's plans and receiving everything He's placed in our hands.

Conclusion

After reading this book you should know that you are not *going* through — you have *come* through. I shall continue praising God for His wonderful works — what He has done and what He is doing and keeps doing in my life.

I'm worshipping Him in spirit and in truth. He's given His Son as a living sacrifice. The price was paid when He allowed Jesus to get up out of the grave. We must obey everyday what He says.

We need to ask Holy Ghost to help us daily to obey God in every way. We should walk in righteousness and decide to live and forgive.

Don't be pressed and pressured by things in life that you can't change. Choose to change in Jesus' name. In his name things shouldn't stay the same.

God hasn't given us the spirit of fear. If we are living in fear we are not living a Christian life. Life is a choice. Choose His voice. Don't ever listen to the voice of the enemy.

Don't have fear, have power, love, and possess a sound mind all the time. Let your light shine with power even in this hour. All things happen within a timeframe of an hour. At the midnight hour, Paul and Silas prayed, and praised.

"Now My soul is troubled and deeply distressed; what shall I say? 'Father, save Me from this hour [of trial and agony]'? But it is for this [very] purpose that I have come to this hour [this time and place]."

JOHN 12:27 AMP

"But about midnight when Paul and Silas were praying and singing hymns of praise to God, and the prisoners were listening to them;

suddenly there was a great earthquake, so [powerful] that the very foundations of the prison were shaken and at once all the doors were opened and everyone's chains were unfastened."

ACTS 16:25-26 AMP

We are receiving today. Every day is a new day to receive. We don't have time to go astray and live any kind of way we choose. We must obey what God says.

Live in love. Choose to love. Love cures many things. Love overrides hate. Live in love for Christ sake. In Christ Jesus is the only way.

Hear, listen, and do what God says to do. This is not an option. It's not about your opinion.

Live in dominion. Be fruitful, multiply, subdue, and replenish. Don't allow your faith to diminish. Don't hold onto what doesn't belong like unforgivenes, depression, oppression, lack, limitations, sickness and disease. Avoid lies, backbiting, jealousy, pride and hatred. These things take you away from the light of Jesus.

Don't look back. Keep pressing forward and receive the blessings God has waiting for you.

Things that keep you down, you can't keep around. Release what you shouldn't keep. Reach far beyond to what you can't see. Faith is receiving what you can't see right now. Soon you will receive it in your life, and in your house.

Make sure you keep learning, obeying, and building up the Kingdom of God. Don't cease to go into the Courts of Heaven and bring back what's needed to enjoy the things right here on earth.

Be a blessing, and live in the blessings now! Rejoice and be exceedingly glad!

A PRAYER OF INTERCESSION FOR ALL PEOPLE

In the name of Jesus. All people are set free.

God's Kingdom has come. His will is being done. Right here on earth, as it is heaven. The heavens are open. God has spoken.

In the name of Jesus, I call and command people to want to obey God, and they will walk in His will. Now. I call and command the lost to be found. In the name of Jesus, I call people to listen to the sound, and know that God is always around.

In the name of Jesus, I command all people to listen and obey, what God has to say every day. In the name of Jesus, I command the captives to be set free. I command, cancel, and curse the devil from the root, from all people, and he flees.

At the name of Jesus every knee bows, and every tongue confesses that Jesus is Lord. God's people will no longer chase decoys.

In the name of Jesus, people will want to be saved, and get saved, because Jesus got up out of the grave.

In the name of Jesus, all will listen to God's voice, make the choice, and rejoice. In the name of Jesus, the joy of the Lord is our strength. Thank God that we have been sent.

In the name of Jesus, we listen and obey when God calls our names. We don't play games. In the name of Jesus, our lives will never be the same. In Christ Jesus we are not ashamed. Victory is our names.

In the name of Jesus, we are strong, and we live long. In the name of Jesus, we live in health, and wealth. In the name of Jesus, we live in the best, we drive the best, we eat the best, we wear the best, and we excel far better than the rest.

In the name of Jesus, we pass all tests. In the name of Jesus, there's no temptation, no tests, no trials, and no tricks of the enemy that can stop us. In God and His Trinity we trust. Serving Him is a must.

In the name of Jesus, we listen closely, follow, and obey Holy Ghost. We preach Jesus from coast to coast. In the name of Jesus, we are blessed indeed, and our territories have been enlarged.

God's hand is on us. We have accepted the command and charge. In the name of Jesus, abundance doesn't have an option, it always has to come to us. In the name of Jesus, abundance doesn't have an opinion, it does what we command it to do, according to the will of God.

In the name of Jesus, abundance keeps on coming to me and you, and we receive. In the name of Jesus, with our wealth, we will help. In the name of Jesus, the world will see that the people of God live large, and they are in charge.

In the name of Jesus, we stand on the rock of our salvation. God is our solid foundation. We bless the nations, generation after generation. In the name of Jesus, we are never put on probation from the world. God has a waiting period without restraints. In the name of Jesus, we never say that we can't.

We confess these scriptures below, out loud every day, and expect something great to happen for us, and through us every day.

This is my prayer. In Jesus name, I pray, believing, trusting and obeying God every day. I command the angels to bring it all to me now. I receive. In Jesus name, amen.

"I can do all things [which He has called me to do] through Him who strengthens and empowers me [to fulfill His purpose—I am self-sufficient in Christ's sufficiency; I am ready for anything and equal to anything through Him who infuses me with inner strength and confident peace.]"

PHILIPPIANS 4:13 AMP

"So now, take your stand and see this great thing which the LORD will do before your eyes."

1 SAMUEL 12:16 AMP

A SNEAK PEEK FROM DREAMS:

Dreams

What Are They & What Do They Mean

Dream

I had a dream Apostle Hilliard was teaching he was stopped by a lady and then went to the back and gave the man some money, came back, and preceded to teach. After he finished teaching, Pastor AD began teaching. He was interrupted by a phone call from the mans wife who received the money from Apostle Hilliard. He stopped and talked to her, and afterwards preceded to teach. God said the most important thing in the Kingdom is the reach and then the teach. Of course, things will be done descent and in order. Holy Ghost order. We must meet the needs of the people. What good is teaching and preaching and no one is helped, or even know what's their next step. The next part of this dream, the lady that interrupted Apostle Hilliard was in the lady's room with me, alone with the man that received the money. She was saying to him, "I told you God would make away." He said, "I believe this stuff now." I told her, "that a man shouldn't be in the lady's room," and they left out. I went back into the sanctuary where pastor AD Hatter was teaching. It was really bright and beautiful in there. As I looked around I said, "this feels nice and looks good in here." It was filled with lots of people. All race, and all kind of people. People were dressed up, some were casual, and some were dressed down. Others looked as though they needed help buying clothes. It was an awesome atmosphere. I said, "God is here." Dream over.

INTERPRETATION

God wants us to come together for His cause and not ours. Recognize who's in our churches, who's in need, and provide help with the need. Show love and kindness, regardless of the race and type of people.

However, we must have money to help people that's in need. Don't be so busy teaching and preaching that you forget what your job in the Kingdom is all about.

Do the work of Jesus. As he went about preaching and teaching he took out time to help those in need. He feed the five thousand women and children. God wants us in place to help the human race. It's not about the color of their face. It's not about how much money they have. Rich or poor He's opened all doors.

Money shall keep coming in, to help us all win. Win the souls. Do as we are told. Watch His blessing unfold. His wisdom from Holy Ghost, we must always behold. We gotta hear from God on every move we make, and every step we take. As long as He allow every breathe, we must walk in faith. We must have insight, and love Him with all our might. We see far beyond what the world sees. We are blessed indeed.

Our coasts have been enlarged. Make sure our reach is far greater than our teach, and preach. Look first, and then we can see what God sees. We must allow Holy Ghost to lead us in the feed. Meet the need. Feed the flock. You can't be blocked or stopped. God's will and work will, and is being done. Do the work we've been called and commanded. Work every hand He's given us. We have received a winners hand. Walk in His plans. He will always allow us to stand. Discerning and knowing what's in the enemy's hand. Again, having insight and faith.

The angels are employed to hear what God, and His people say. They bring all His promises to us every day. The heavens are opened. God has spoken. Receive our fullness, fruitfulness, fatness, and fountains with a continual flow. We will now begin to walk in health and wealth like never before. Obey, and stay in place. Always be ready to be used by God at all times. Your lights will continue to shine all the time. Keep walking in His Divine. His Trinity.

If you enjoyed this book, please check out Lady Mary's other books:

The Secrets Are Out:
Nothing Happens Until the Secrets Are Revealed!

This powerful and awesome book will allow you to live and love life. Even though you might face troubled situations in life, God has allowed you to know what His Word says about it. You can come through everything that comes against you, when you obey what He says to do. God's secrets revealed are for you to rest, reign, rule, remain, and receive.

Book of Revelations: Divine Disclosures of Best Kept Secrets!:

This is another awesome book of revealed secrets from God, which He has blessed me to write, and I know it will bless the body of Christ. Believers must believe these two key truths: 1) God is NOT a man. 2) God DOES NOT lie.

T.S.I.T.S.: Things Seen in the Spirit

God is so awesome! He has allowed me to hear from Him like never before. As I pray daily and communicate with God and begin to listen to Him; He shares secrets with me to be revealed to the world. First God speaks what He wants to happen, how He wants it done and who He wants to do His work.

Confessions Journal: God's Word Spoken in Faith, Believing that He Will Bring it to Pass,
According to His Will for Our Lives:

Lady Mary Hatter's writing will inspire you, as she shares secrets from God through confessions spoken to her by His Spirit... Confessions from this book will help you to receive everything you want in the Kingdom and everything you want in every area of your life, your family and friend's lives.

God's Decrees Spoken By Me, I Receive!
Thank You Lord, for the Increase!

This awesome book of Decrees will teach you what to speak and how to receive. This book allows you to speak His promotions, promises, provisions, peace and prosperity. This book also speaks revelations, restoration, redemption, and helps reassign and realign things in your life.

In this book you will learn how to live and love life by speaking out your mouths what God says, and do what He says do, so that all His blessings shall keep coming to you. We decree manifestations, because we are a blessed generation and generations to come. It is God's will being done. Decrees are for our victory, and for all the world to see. We have His-story! We are made in His image. So is Jesus, so are we: because of His Decrees, we can and will live in prosperity! Receive all these Decrees!

Water Breaking Faith:
The Aftermath of Hurricane Harvey's Path

Praise God! I'm so overwhelmed with joy; even though the enemy sent a decoy. God's people are being led and fed by His Spirit, therefore the devil can't destroy.

As we continue to walk in willingness and obedience, we continue to eat the good of the land. We can never be destroyed by the pestilence and predators in these perilous times of the present, and the things that's coming. Know that victory has already been won, because of God's precious son!

You will be inspired and know how to acquire, access, and possess from God: and follow His instructions. After reading and listening to Lady Mary's journey of going through Hurricane Harvey and it's aftermath, you will be imparted with much information on how she, her husband, daughter, and grandchildren triumphed in all they went through.

To God be the glory!

Dreams: What Are They and What Do They Mean?

This is a book of dreams, and interpretations. God has revealed these dreams to His prophets. They are revelations from Holy Ghost. Here are some questions about dreams and you'll receive the answers after Holy Spirit reveals them to me.

Are you dreaming big or small? In you dreams do you continue to fall? Do your dreams seem to be off the wall? In your dreams are you standing tall? Holy Spirit has revealed them all!

Dreams aren't just for sleepers, but they are for reapers! You can receive your big dreams if you choose to believe! Believe the prophet so shall you prosper. Our dreams have meaning. We must know what God has already given us, even in the beginning. Dreams are a blessing.

Dreams come with a message and a lesson. Never give up on your dreams. God allows you to dream, and know what they mean. Listen, and hear the message. Learn the lesson. Obey and do; watch God give them all to you.

Dream BIG!

    <u>B</u>lessings.
    <u>I</u>mpartation.
    <u>G</u>od given

Follow your dreams, stay faithful and focused! Know that God has already made the way. Your dreams shall come to pass. Your blessings from God will always last.

Invite Christian Teacher
Lady Mary Hatter
to speak at your church or event

Lady Mary helps people walk in their purpose; which is to build up the Kingdom of God first, and then they can live effective, efficient, and excellent lives, in order to experience all that God has already promised them.

Life Coaching and Author Coaching services are also available.

Follow her on social media:

Facebook: Upe Deisgns Tsits
Twitter: @LadyMaryHatter
Instagram: LadyMaryHatter
Amazon: Click her author page and follow her

To book Lady Mary, please call
281.254.5994
or visit her website and fill out the contact form.

www.MaryHatter.com

www.ingramcontent.com/pod-product-compliance
Lightning Source LLC
Chambersburg PA
CBHW070114080526
44586CB00013B/1291